Grade 5

Scott Foresman
Readers' Theater Anthology

D1543848

PEARSON

Scott Foresman

Editorial Offices: Glenview, Illinois • Parsippany, New Jersey • New York, New York
Sales Offices: Needham, Massachusetts • Duluth, Georgia • Glenview, Illinois
Coppell, Texas • Sacramento, California • Mesa, Arizona

Acknowledgments

Poetry

P4 "The Brave Ones" by Eloise Greenfield from *Under the Sunday Tree* by Eloise Greenfield. Copyright © 1988 by Eloise Greenfield. Used by permission of HarperCollins Publishers.

P6 "How to Assemble a Toy" from *Mummy Took Cooking Lessons* by John Ciardi. Text copyright © 1990 by Judith C. Ciardi. Reprinted by permission of Houghton Mifflin Company. All rights reserved.

P7 "The Basket Weaver," from *Remember the Bridge: Poems of a People* by Carole Boston Weatherford, copyright © 2002 by Carole Boston Weatherford, text. Used by permission of Philomel Books, A Division of Penguin Young Readers Group, A Member of Penguin Group (USA) Inc., 345 Hudson Street, New York, NY 10014. All rights reserved.

P8 "Changing" by Mary Ann Hoberman from *The Llama Who Had No Pajama*. Copyright © 1998 by Mary Ann Hoberman. Reprinted by permission of Houghton Mifflin Company. All rights reserved.

P9 "Early Explorers" from *Footprints on the Roof: Poems About the Earth* by Marilyn Singer illustrated by Meilo So, copyright © 2002 by Marilyn Singer. Illustrations copyright © 2002 by Meilo So. Used by permission of Alfred A. Knopf, an imprint of Random House Children's Books, a division of Random House, Inc.

P10 "Always Take a Dog" from *The World According to Dog: Poems and Teen Voices* by Joyce Sidman. Poetry copyright © 2003 by Joyce Sidman. Reprinted by permission of Houghton Mifflin Company. All rights reserved.

P15 "Celebration" by Alonzo Lopez, from *Whispering Wind* by Terry Allen, copyright © 1972 by the Institute of American Indian Arts. Used by permission of Doubleday, a division of Random House, Inc.

Contents

© Pearson Education 5

Practice with a Purpose

by Sam Sebesta

As indicated in the directions in this book, Readers' Theater is a performance activity with a simple format. Costumes, makeup, and scenery are not required. Action is minimal. Because scripts are used, there's no lengthy time spent memorizing lines.

The goal is a shared oral reading performance that rocks the rafters, whether an audience is present or not. People with long memories compare it to radio drama in days of old. Yet there's nothing out-of-date about Readers' Theater. Its benefits are recognized by modern researchers. Listen to this:

ABOUT THE AUTHOR
Sam Sebesta is a Professor Emeritus from the College of Education at the University of Washington in Seattle. He continues to write and do research in children's literature, decoding in linguistic development, oral reading fluency, and reader response.

TEACHER *(puzzled):* Why are we doing Readers' Theater?

READING PROFESSOR *(reading from a scholarly paper):* "Readers' Theater promotes fluency and expression as a result of repeated reading and encouragement to make the performance sound natural and meaningful."

STUDENT 1 *(aside):* Will that be on the test?

No, that won't be on the test, although it's a good rationale for teachers to know about. Beyond this, it might be beneficial to discuss the reasons for Readers' Theater with your class.

TEACHER *(still puzzled):* Why are we doing Readers' Theater?

STUDENT 2: Because it's fun.

STUDENT 3: Because you learn to get the words right.

STUDENT 4: You learn to speak up so others can hear you.

STUDENT 5 *(the reflective one):* It's good for the imagination.

Good reasons, all. Here are five more, gleaned from comments during Readers' Theater classes and workshops:

"You get practice with a purpose."

The purpose, of course, is to present a worthy performance. The practice? It begins the moment scripts are passed out. It continues as students take their parts home or to a quiet corner to practice their lines. It flourishes in group rehearsal.

"You learn to make it sound like people talking."

A smooth delivery—flow of language, not word-by-word—is an objective in Readers' Theater that students can understand. How to achieve it? Practice reading a line and then look up and say it directly to another character. Pretty soon the fluency will come.

"More of you get to read at one time."

In this student's class, several groups are rehearsing their scripts simultaneously before they come together to perform for each other. The ratio of readers to listeners is higher than you'd find in classes where one reads and all others listen. Hence, there's more practice, more involvement.

"You learn to get into character."

Sounds too grown-up? Not at all! Children realize, from the start, that the way to portray Chicken Little is to try running like Chicken Little and talking like Chicken Little. Using mime and made-up speeches to help "get into character" may be a useful device to prepare for Readers' Theater. And there may be a more lasting payoff: readers who enjoy reading often see themselves in the roles of the characters they're reading about.

"It's reading you get to do with your friends."

Avid readers, when interviewed, speak frequently about the social value of reading, praising reading activities that have them interacting with peers. Non-avid readers who think of reading as a lonely task may also find that interactive activities such as Readers' Theater and Choral Reading alter attitudes toward the positive.

These, then, are benefits you may discover from Readers' Theater and Choral Reading. There may be more. The effects of good oral reading may be internalized, resulting in improved silent reading. Hence, speaking and listening to complex style, dialogue in character, and other features of print contribute to effective silent reading. It's no coincidence that avid readers (i.e., children and young adults who read voluntarily an hour or more a day) cite reading aloud and being read to as the major factor leading to their success.

With all these reasons in mind, Scott Foresman Reading Street offers you the directions and selections in this book. We hope you enjoy them. We want you to find them useful as a component of a powerful reading program.

Readers' Theater in Your Classroom

by Alisha Fran-Potter

Staging the Play

ACTING AREA

If you don't have a stage at your disposal, your classroom will work fine. First you need to define a functional acting area. This could be the front or back of the room with some or all of the desks pushed out of the way. It could be a taped-off area on the floor. If you need or want to leave all your desks in place, you will need enough space in front of the room for students to stand in a row. Once you decide what will work best for your class and room layout, explain to your students and train them how to prepare the acting area when you give the signal.

ABOUT THE AUTHOR
Alisha Fran-Potter is a Drama Specialist with the Glenview, Illinois, public schools. She has taught in classrooms at grades K, 1, and 2, and speech, drama, and language arts at grades 6, 7, and 8.

MOVEMENT AND BLOCKING

Traditionally, Readers' Theater is performed with the actors seated on chairs or stools in a row facing the audience, with their scripts in their hands or on stands in front of them. Actors do not memorize their parts but read them or at least refer to their scripts as they act. In this traditional method, actors do not look at each other but keep their focus out front. You can include movement in your production or not. Decide before you start how much movement there will be. Keep in mind that if students have scripts in their hands, their movements must be limited. If they remain in place, they might gesture with one free hand.

Any movement about the stage you have the actors do is called *blocking.* Your blocking choices depend on your acting area. If you have the space and want to have your actors move about freely, do so. However, if your acting area is limited, keep the blocking simple, perhaps just having the actors move from one chair to another, cross the stage, or come and go in the acting area.

If the actors are up and moving around, you need to consider their focus (whom they are talking to), and angle (the direction they face). Actors should not face each other directly, but rather turn their bodies slightly toward the audience. This is called *cheating,* and if done well it can look perfectly natural. In cheating positions, two actors would position their bodies at about 90° to each other.

If there is a place that remains the same throughout the story, such as a house or a lake, you might tape an area out on the floor or block it off with chairs or markers. This way all actors know where the place is within the acting area. You can designate entrances and exits in the same way.

ENTRANCES AND EXITS

For a smooth-running performance, rehearse entrances and exits when you rehearse the play.

- Actors can all enter at the same time, go to their assigned places, and then all exit at the same time. Or, they can all be "discovered" by lights up at the beginning—with lights down to signal the end.

- Actors can enter as their characters come into the story and then stay or leave and come back. You will need to decide if all the actors stay on stage after their parts are finished. (If they remain, they can all share a curtain call.)

- Actors can remain at their desks until it is their turn to perform, do their roles, and then go back to their seats. This works only if your classroom is big enough to accommodate a seating area and separate acting area.

ASSIGNING PARTS

Plan in advance how parts will be assigned and explain the process to your students. Some ways to do this are:

Volunteers This method allows students to volunteer for the parts they are interested in. Go though all the parts and describe them if necessary. Then explain that when you ask who is interested in playing each part they should raise their hands. Suggest that students have second and third choices in mind because they won't always get their first choices. If you know that a volunteer can't handle a specific part for whatever reason, choose another student and give the first student a more appropriate part. This works better with some groups than with other groups, and you must assess your students' abilities to handle volunteering.

Draw Markers To assign parts randomly, make up sticks with the student's names on them. Choose a stick and assign that person the part that is up next. This works well if all the parts are about the same in length and difficulty—and if the parts are gender-neutral. You will have to use your discretion, however, to avoid choosing a student who can't handle the reading of a role because it is large or because it will embarrass the student for some reason.

Teacher Choice Do this ahead of time to save class time. Simply go through the cast list and the student list and decide who will play what part. This works well—and indeed may be necessary—if there are varied abilities in the class and the roles vary much in length. But you must know your students and the parts in the play well in order to use this method.

Audition Students can do a cold reading from the script, or they can be given time to prepare. Preparation time could vary from five minutes to a class period or the next day. Depending on the ages of the students, you can choose the passages for audition or let the students choose. This method works if you have a large amount of time for the play or a number of periods for preparation and rehearsal.

SCENERY AND PROPS

Scenery provides the setting—where the story takes place. If you have access to a curtain backdrop, use it by all means. Chances are, however, that you are stuck with a wall of your classroom. If you have the space, you might be able to arrange desks, tables, carts, easels, chairs, and so on to suggest a setting. You might consider having students create a scene in colored chalk on your chalkboard. Keep in mind, however, that the best scenery is created in the imaginations of your audience.

Props are anything the actors handle. Traditional Readers' Theater uses no props, but if you choose to use props, keep them simple. Remember that the actors still have to manipulate their scripts. If the play calls for a bag or a purse, the actor can use a backpack or coat. Other ordinary classroom items that can serve as props include: books, clipboards, pencil cases, boxes, book ends, pens or pencils, paper, note cards, notebooks, cups, vases, water bottles.

Adapting Scripts

Ideally, every student in a class or group will have his or her own role in Readers' Theater. If these scripts have too many or too few roles for your class, you may need to adapt them to fit. To reduce characters:

- Eliminate parts that are redundant or not vital to the plot. For example, reduce four narrators to two by having Narrator 1 read lines designated Narrator 1 and Narrator 3, and so on.

- Take out parts with animal sounds or cheering crowds and just let the audience infer them.

- Characters with single lines or few lines can be doubled by actors who aren't in the same scene.

- Perform only scenes for which you have enough actors. You can summarize or narrate missing scenes that are needed to get the story across.

To add characters:

- If there are many Narrator lines, divide them up to allow for more narrators.

- Have two students play a role at the same time. If there is a cat in the story, turn it into two cats. They can alternate lines or recite them in unison.

- Add a counterpart character and have them say their lines together or divide the lines. For example, if there is a Queen in the story, create a King.

- If there is a part such as Townsperson, turn it into Townspeople and have more than one actor read it simultaneously.

- If many extra parts are needed, cast by scene. For example, have different actors play the King in Scene 1 and Scene 2.

Note that the suggestions for simultaneous reading also work well to help students with special needs or ELL students who are just learning English.

Adapting Trade Books for Readers' Theater

You can adapt any kind of book into a Readers' Theater script. But not every story is equally suited to the stage. Look for a story with a strong narrative line. An easy-to-follow plot adapts more effectively than a plot or story line that is too complex. If it feels complicated, you might need to simplify the plot somehow. Even nonfiction books can be turned into scripts, but among those, the books with strong narrative lines—such as biography or history—will be most effective. Here are some further elements to consider:

Narration When you are adapting your script, first eliminate all speech tags, such as "he said" and "Josefina replied." Eliminate lengthy descriptions. If you feel some description is necessary, try to put it in the mouth of a character who has a reason to describe something.

Narrators can be very useful, but try to keep their function to introducing, enhancing, or moving the story along. Sometimes they may be necessary to make transitions between scenes. However, don't rely on narrators to tell the story. For example, don't write:

NARRATOR: It is early Monday morning. Mary is eagerly waiting for friends to look at her garden before the judges come. Finally Tessa arrives.

MARY: I'll show you my flowers.

NARRATOR: Together they walk to the garden in back of the house. They see beautiful bright yellow sunflowers and blazing red poppies.

Aim to show, not to tell. In other words, dramatize, don't narrate. For example, you might write:

NARRATOR: It is early Monday morning. Mary is eagerly waiting.

MARY: Good morning, Tessa!

TESSA: Hi, Mary. I've come to see that award-winning garden of yours.

MARY: I hope. But I'm glad you could come before the judges get here.

TESSA: So am I. I can't wait to see what you've done this year. I hear it's beautiful and full of color.

MARY: Oh, it is! I have bright yellow sunflowers and blazing red poppies. Here, let me show you. It's out back. Follow me.

You will find that it is helpful to have characters repeat each other's names often. This helps the audience keep track of who is speaking, especially when there are a lot of characters in a scene.

Dialogue Look at the dialogue in a book to see how much there is. Some dialogue you might be able to use directly in your script. Some you may need to simplify or pare down. Some dialogue you may decide to break up into smaller units, so that one character doesn't talk for too long at one time.

Be sure that the dialogue is appropriate for the age group you're working with. If not, you may be able to make it more appropriate by substitution, elimination, or addition.

If you are creating new dialogue, be sure it is in the voice of the character; that is, appropriate to that character's age, education, sophistication, and so on.

Repetition Repetition may be of actions or of language. Repetition of actions allows actors—and the audience—to follow the story line more easily. For example, the First Pig builds a house of straw, the Second Pig builds a house of twigs, and the Third Pig builds a house of bricks.

Repetition of language might be a repeated phrase or sentence such as the Wolf's line, "I'll huff and I'll puff and I'll blow your house down!" which he says before his attack on each Pig's house.

Younger children especially do well with repetition, but don't discount its effectiveness even for the older grades. Many elaborate folk tales develop their plot lines through the use of repetition.

Group Characters These allow for multiple roles. For example, if you have twenty-six actors, with one main character and five supporting characters, all can have a role. One or two actors can play the main character, and then several actors can play each of the supporting characters. For example, take the story *Anansi and the Moss-Covered Rock* by Eric Kimmel.

© Pearson Education 5

Anansi, the spider, is walking though the forest when he finds a magic rock. He uses this rock to trick his friends so he can take their food. Little Bush Deer won't let Anansi fool him, though, and teaches Anansi a lesson in turn.

One or two actors can play Anansi, one or two can play the rock, and the rest of the actors can be divided among the other animals. So you might have three or four Lions, Elephants, Rhinoceroses, Hippopotamuses, Giraffes, Zebras, and Little Bush Deers.

Special Effects

You can create effective Readers' Theater using nothing but the actors' voices. However, if you want to add to the theatrical experience, consider the following:

MUSIC

You can use recorded or live music (such as a piano or guitar) to make transitions between scenes, to show the passage of time, or for background to heighten the mood. Be sure that the music is appropriate to the mood and pace of the scene. If you are using recorded music, practice cueing it up during rehearsals.

LIGHTING

If you are working on a stage with a lighting system, you can either open the curtain or bring the lights up on your actors already in place. If the actors must take their places in view of the audience, you can dim the lights to black and then bring them up to signal the start of the performance.

SOUND EFFECTS

Remember that the actors themselves can create all the sound effects with their voices alone. However, here are some additional suggestions for these plays.

Puss in Boots Of course the actor playing the Ogre will want to roar as a lion and squeak as a mouse, but it might add to the audience's amusement if he roared into a megaphone or some kind of public-address system.

Knocks in the Night Sybil can have a piece of wood to pound on a wooden desk or chair.

Ro Bo Cleaner Ro and Bo can be played by two actors, or you can assign a small chorus to make their noises. Ro Bo's noises can continue under the other speeches, but don't let them take over the play.

Adventure by the Barrel Water noises can be added orally by a number of actors in concert. Annie Taylor can make her voice sound hollow when she is in the barrel by speaking into a large hollow cardboard tube.

About the Playwrights

Jane Boyd Wendling wrote the book for the musical *Charlie's Oasis,* which was produced in Chicago and Omsk, Russia. She also wrote the book for the children's musical *Hans Brinker and the Silver Skates,* also produced in Chicago and by Pandora's Playhouse in Rushville, Illinois. Ms. Wendling wrote both book and music for *Reunion,* a history-based pageant commissioned by the Scripps family of newspaper publishers.

Don Abramson wrote *Melissa, While She Sleeps,* a collection of poems that was staged in Phoenix, Chicago, New York, and London, England. He has written several short plays for children that were published in reading textbooks. He wrote the books and lyrics for two children's musicals, *The Well of the Guelphs,* which was produced in Lincoln, Nebraska, and Okoboji, Iowa, and *Who Is Cinderella?* which was commissioned by Chicago's Duncan YMCA.

Alisha Fran-Potter is a Drama Specialist with Glenview (IL) School District 34. She has her BS in Education and her Masters in Curriculum and Instruction, with an emphasis in Fine Arts. She has taught Kindergarten, 1st and 2nd grade, Drama for grades K–8, and Drama and Speech for grades 6–8. Mrs. Fran-Potter developed, wrote, and implemented fine arts curriculums for Districts 34 and 81. She has presented at the Illinois Reading Council and taught for Glenview University.

Maggie Gautier is a writer, humorist, and songwriter who has been writing, producing, and performing her one-woman shows in Chicago for over a decade. She is a student of musical theater and a member of Theatre Building Chicago's Writers' Workshop. She collaborated on the musical *To Bee or Not to Bee.* Ms. Gautier works as a film producer and sales representative for a film production company.

Peter Grahame has written Readers' Theater scripts for community projects as well as educational materials for young people. He has acted in or directed community, academic, and professional theatrical productions in many cities across the country. He is also an artist and a photographer. His short play "In Search of Wisdom" was published in a reading textbook.

Cynthia Gallaher studied screenwriting and also studied oral interpretation at St. Nicholas Theater Company. She wrote the script for the mini-musical "Can't Help but Dance" in Theatre Building Chicago Writers' Workshop. She was awarded a Community Arts Assistance Program Grant in Theater from the City of Chicago, and she is currently writing the book and lyrics for a children's musical, *Xavier and the White Cat.*

Puss in Boots

based on a fairy tale
by Charles Perrault

by Jane Boyd Wendling

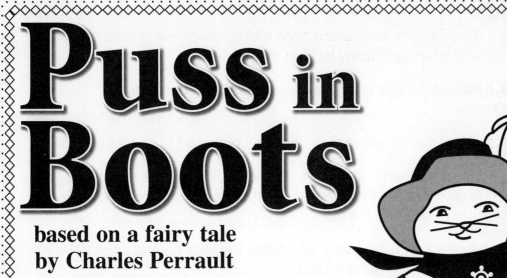

CHARACTERS

ABRAHAM, the oldest son
BERTRAM, the second son
CHESTER, the youngest son
PUSS IN BOOTS
HAZEL, the King's Butler
KING
HAROLD, the King's Driver
ANNABELLE, the Princess
FARMER 1
FARMER 2
HILDA, the Ogre's Manager
OGRE
NARRATORS 1–4

A cat doesn't seem like
much of an inheritance,
but the animal proves
far more valuable
than anyone realizes.

NARRATOR 1 In a faraway land, there once lived a Miller. He ground the farmers' wheat into flour, making a good living.

NARRATOR 2 Now this Miller had three sons: Abraham, Bertram, and Chester.

NARRATOR 3 When the old Miller died, the sons gathered to share his estate.

ABRAHAM Well, my brothers, our father is dead and buried. All he had, he has left to us—the mill, his savings, and the donkey. As the oldest son, I will naturally take over the mill.

BERTRAM And I will claim the donkey, Abraham. Perhaps he and I can deliver grain from the mill to your customers!

ABRAHAM That might work out well, Bertram. And you and I will divide the savings. Sorry, Chester: we outrank you.

CHESTER Do I get nothing, then?

ABRAHAM Let's see—well, there IS Father's pussycat! You can have that.

CHESTER The pussycat! What on earth can I do with a cat?

ABRAHAM He's a wonderful cat—very fat and sleek.

CHESTER Sure. I'll eat him as my last meal—before I starve to death.

BERTRAM Good luck, anyway, Chester! Come, Abraham—we'll plan our business.

PUSS (*after a pause*) You're not really going to eat me, are you, Chester?

CHESTER What? Who said that?!

PUSS Do you see anyone else who was just threatened with being eaten?

CHESTER Is that you, Puss? You can TALK?

PUSS Obviously.

CHESTER But you've been around for years, and I never heard you talk before.

PUSS Nobody ever threatened to eat me before, either.

CHESTER I wouldn't really have eaten you. But how are we going to live?

PUSS I have a few ideas.

CHESTER Come to think of it, I have seen you do some clever tricks.

PUSS I've got tricks you've never dreamed of! Tell you what—get me a bag and a pair of boots. You'll see you haven't done so badly after all!

NARRATOR 4 So Chester went into the village, and found a shoemaker who would make a pair of very small boots, just right for Puss.

CHESTER Here they are, Puss—boots, just your size!

PUSS Very nice! They fit perfectly! How do I look?

CHESTER Quite dashing. I think from now on I shall call you Puss in Boots!

PUSS Puss in Boots—I like it! What about the bag?

CHESTER Will this bag do? It has a drawstring so you can close it tightly.

PUSS That will do nicely!

SCENE 2

NARRATOR 1 So Puss took the bag and went out to hunt for rabbits.

NARRATOR 2 He put some crisp, green lettuce into the bag and stretched out beside it as if he were having a nap.

NARRATOR 3 Soon a young rabbit came along, smelled the good stuff in the bag, and hopped in after it.

NARRATOR 4 Quick as a wink, Puss in Boots pulled the drawstring tight and trapped the rabbit in the bag. He hurried off to the royal palace, where the Butler met him at the door.

HAZEL Not so fast there, cat. What are you doing here?

PUSS I'm here to see the King. Is anything wrong with that?

HAZEL Well, we don't get too many cats around here that can talk! I'll find out if His Majesty wants to see you.

NARRATOR 1 The Butler turned around and headed for the King's chamber.

HAZEL Your Majesty, there is a cat at the door asking to see you!

KING A talking cat? That might be amusing. Show him in!

NARRATOR 2 So the Butler showed Puss into the King's chamber.

PUSS Your Majesty, I have here a fine rabbit sent to you by my Lord, the—er—the Duke of Carabas (KAIR uh bahs).

KING A rabbit? How very thoughtful. I shall have the royal Chef prepare it for my lunch. Please extend my thanks to your master.

SCENE 3

NARRATOR 3 Next day Puss went out again with his bag. This time he baited it with grain, lay down, and pretended to take a nap.

NARRATOR 4 Soon along came a fine fat partridge, who saw the grain in the open bag and went in after it.

NARRATOR 1 And sly Puss in Boots quickly drew the string tight, and the partridge was caught. Again he hurried to the royal palace.

PUSS *(calling out)* Yoo-hoo! Madame Butler!

HAZEL Watch out, cat, or you'll make a nuisance of yourself. And for your information, my name is Hazel.

PUSS Okay, Hazel. Just tell the King I'm here. I'm sure he'll want to see me.

NARRATOR 2 So Puss was again admitted to the King's chamber.

PUSS Greetings, Your Majesty! I have another gift for you from the Duke of Carabas. Fine rare birds such as this thickly flock his lands.

KING Thank you, Cat.

PUSS I'm called Puss in Boots, Sire, on account of my lovely boots.

KING Yes, I wondered about those. Goodbye, now. *(To himself.)* Strange—I've never heard of this Duke of Carabas. He must be important, though.

SCENE 4

NARRATOR 3 Day after day, Puss in Boots brought gifts for the King. And the King came to believe that the Duke of Carabas must be very rich indeed!

NARRATOR 4 One day Puss ran into Hazel, the King's Butler, on the road.

PUSS Good day, Hazel.

HAZEL Good day, Puss. Do you have gifts for my master again?

PUSS Not today, friend. How is your master, the King?

HAZEL Oh, he's quite well. In fact, he's planning to take his daughter, the Princess, for a drive along the river today.

PUSS A princess? I didn't know there WAS a princess!

HAZEL She's rarely permitted outside the castle, because the King loves her so dearly. He's afraid some local youth might be bewitched by her beauty and fall in love. Even worse, the Princess might fall in love with such a fellow.

PUSS So, would that be a bad thing?

HAZEL His Majesty thinks so. Only the very handsomest and richest man in the world would be suitable for the King's daughter.

PUSS Of course. That would be only right and proper. Goodbye, Hazel.

NARRATOR 1 So Puss hurried back home and found Chester.

PUSS Listen up, Chester, if you do as I say, you'll make your fortune.

CHESTER My fortune? I'm just happy you've been bringing home enough game to put food on the table and keep us alive!

PUSS We'll do much better than that. I've only been bringing home the small stuff. Can you guess where the fine game has gone?

CHESTER The fine game? You mean bigger, fatter rabbits?

PUSS Not just rabbits, Chester. Partridges, quail, and other delicious tidbits. And do you know what I've been doing with them?

CHESTER I haven't the slightest idea.

PUSS Well, I've been taking these wonderful gifts to the King.

CHESTER The KING? You mean they let you in the palace? InSIDE the palace?

PUSS I'm practically a regular there.

CHESTER I can't believe it!

PUSS Believe it. AND—here's what we're going to do next. Actually, what YOU're going to do.

CHESTER Me?

PUSS You indeed! I want you to go swimming in the river just as I tell you.

CHESTER Me? Go swimming? In the river?

PUSS Chester, you've got to pull your own weight a LITTLE!

NARRATOR 2 So Chester went down to the river and went in swimming at the place Puss showed him. While he was swimming, Puss took his shabby clothes and hid them away.

NARRATOR 3 When the King's carriage came near, Puss ran to the road crying—

PUSS Help! Help! The Duke of Carabas is drowning!

NARRATOR 4 And the King, recognizing Puss, barked out an order to his Driver.

KING Go at once to the Duke's aid, Harold. Save him from drowning!

NARRATOR 1 Harold made a beeline to the river, jumped in, and pulled the Duke—our Chester—to shore. Sopping wet, Harold returned to the King.

HAROLD *(gasping for breath)* Sire . . . I pulled him out of the river!

KING Yes, thank you, Harold. But it seems the Duke has no manners. Does he not wish to thank me himself?

HAROLD Perhaps, Sire, he doesn't want to meet the King in his underwear.

PUSS He's right! While the Duke was swimming, some rogue stole his clothes!

KING We can take care of that. Harold! Go to the palace at once and fetch a suit of clothes—something suitable for a rich nobleman.

PUSS Oh, yes! That is very generous of Your Majesty.

NARRATOR 2 So Harold brought back a suit of clothes, much finer than Chester had ever even seen.

NARRATOR 3 Chester dressed and came to the carriage to meet the King.

CHESTER Oh, Your Majesty, I thank you for your kindness.

KING You are quite welcome, my son.

ANNABELLE Father, aren't you going to introduce me to the young man?

KING Introduce you? *(Aside.)* Oh, I suppose I must. *(Aloud, to all.)* Daughter, I wish to present the Duke of Carabas.

CHESTER Where? Who is—?

PUSS *(privately, to Chester)* You fool, that's you!

CHESTER Me? Oh—!

KING Duke, may I present my daughter—Princess Annabelle.

CHESTER Good day, my Lady.

ANNABELLE Good day, sir. I'm so glad you were rescued from the river.

CHESTER Thank you. And thanks to you, Your Majesty, for providing this beautiful suit of clothes.

ANNABELLE They become you well! *(Privately, to the King.)* Father, I do believe this is the most handsome young man I've ever met—not that I've met very many.

KING Indeed you have not—I've seen to that. And perhaps I've made a mistake in permitting you to meet THIS one!

ANNABELLE Oh, no! This was no mistake. In fact, I wonder if fate hasn't brought him to us! I do believe I've fallen in love with him—instantly!

CHESTER In love? With me?

ANNABELLE Oh, did you overhear me? Well, then I must admit—yes!

CHESTER You are indeed very beautiful. I think I could love you as well!

PUSS *(aside)* Oh, I am a sly puss! This is even better than I expected!

KING Come, daughter. We must be on our way to the palace.

ANNABELLE Father dear, couldn't the Duke of Carabas ride with us?

KING Annabelle, you know I can't refuse you anything! Very well. Carabas?

NARRATOR 4 So Chester—the Duke of Carabas—climbed into the carriage.

PUSS Please excuse me, Your Majesties, I must attend to some cat business.

SCENE 6

NARRATOR 1 Puss bowed low, then turned around and sped away. Far ahead on the road, he came upon some farmers in a field.

PUSS Good farmers! The royal carriage is coming this way! Help me play a trick on the King. When he asks you who owns these fields, tell him the Duke of Carabas! Do as I tell you, and I'll reward you handsomely.

FARMER 1 But sir, these lands belong to the wicked Ogre, who lives in that castle. If we make one false move, he might turn into a snake and bite us!

FARMER 2 Or become an angry bear and tear us limb from limb!

PUSS I know all about that nasty old Ogre and his bag of tricks. Just relax. If my plan works, I'll rid you of him forever.

NARRATOR 2 When the royal coach drew near, it stopped at that very field.

HAROLD Good farmers! The King wishes to know who owns these fields.

FARMER 1 The Duke of Carabas, sir. He has owned them for—er—

FARMER 2 Quite a long time!

PUSS (aside) My plan is working! We'll be rich by nightfall!

NARRATOR 3 Rubbing his paws with glee, Puss walked boldly to the very door of the Ogre's castle.

PUSS (loudly) I have a message for the owner of this castle!

HILDA Please keep your voice down!

PUSS You don't look at all like an ogre.

HILDA I beg your pardon! I'm not an ogre—I'm Hilda, the castle Manager.

PUSS I do apologize, Hilda. Now please take me to your master.

HILDA Oh, I don't know. We're so busy today—you see, there's to be a banquet. On the other hand, a talking cat might just amuse my master, the Ogre, and put him in a better mood. Very well, come along.

SCENE 7

NARRATOR 4 So Hilda led Puss in Boots into the castle to meet the Ogre.

HILDA Master, this—cat—wishes to speak to you.

OGRE A cat? Well, this is unusual indeed. Good day, cat.

PUSS I'm called Puss in Boots, sir. I've heard so much about you that I simply had to pay you a visit. I can't believe the things I hear are true. It is said, for example, that you can change yourself into any sort of creature, such as a lion or an elephant! Surely you can't change yourself into a lion!

OGRE Oh, indeed I can. To prove it, I shall now become a lion! *(Roaring, as a lion.)* What do you think of me now, cat? Perhaps I shall just eat you up as an appetizer! *(Roaring again.)*

PUSS Oh, my! I am indeed impressed! You are one of the biggest lions I have ever seen! Although, come to think of it, I have never truly SEEN a lion before.

OGRE Well, you have seen one now! How dare you question my power?

PUSS Please sir, do change back into your kindly ogre self.

OGRE Very well. Being a lion is quite taxing. *(Lesser roars, as he gradually becomes himself again.)* There, you see, I'm just a good fellow, after all.

PUSS Indeed you are. And I believe that you can do nearly anything you choose.

OGRE I can.

PUSS Except, of course, for one thing. I've heard you can change yourself into the tiniest of creatures, even a mouse. Surely that's impossible.

OGRE Impossible? You shall see. Before your very eyes, I shall turn myself into a mouse! *(Squeaking, as a mouse.)* See! Now I wouldn't frighten a fruit fly.

PUSS Marvelous! Of course I, myself, am not at all afraid of mice. In fact—I find them extremely tasty—! Meowerrow!

NARRATOR 1 Of course, you can guess the fate of the tiny mouse that the Ogre had become.

PUSS *(smacking his lips)* I must say, this is working out even better than I expected! A fine dinner for me in the bargain!

SCENE 8

NARRATOR 2 Just then the King's carriage was passing the Ogre's castle.

KING This castle looks very fine. Let's stop and rest for a moment.

NARRATOR 3 So Harold turned the carriage onto the road to the castle.

NARRATOR 4 Hearing the carriage on the road, Puss went out to meet it.

PUSS Your Majesty! Welcome to the castle of my lord Duke of Carabas!

KING The Duke, you say? So this castle belongs to you, Carabas?

CHESTER I—ah—Yes, I—ah—I guess—

PUSS The Duke warmly invites Your Majesties into his home!

NARRATOR 1 After Puss had given Chester a shove, that noble figure offered his hand to the Princess, and they followed the King and Puss into the great hall.

PUSS It seems that you were expected, Your Majesty. As you can see, a fine banquet has been prepared.

ANNABELLE Oh, Father—the Duke of Carabas is not only handsome, and good, but very rich and generous! I am more in love with him every minute!

CHESTER And I with you, lovely lady. I'm probably dreaming, but if that's the case, I hope I never wake up.

KING You seem a fine young man. I can see quite easily why my daughter is so taken with you. My lord Duke, would you like to become my son-in-law?

CHESTER How could anyone refuse such an offer? Of course I accept!

NARRATOR 2 Right then and there, the King performed the marriage ceremony uniting the young couple.

PUSS Sire! Guests are arriving to share the wedding banquet!

NARRATOR 3 And so they did. If they were surprised to be welcomed by the King, the Princess Annabelle, somebody called the Duke of Carabas, and a talking cat, instead of the Ogre who had invited them, they were polite enough not to mention it.

NARRATOR 4 And they all lived happily ever after.

PUSS Especially me! Now you know how a clever cat like yours truly can bring fortune to his master. And—I haven't done badly, myself! *(Calling out.)* Servant! Another roasted partridge, please!

KNOCKS in the NIGHT

by Don Abramson

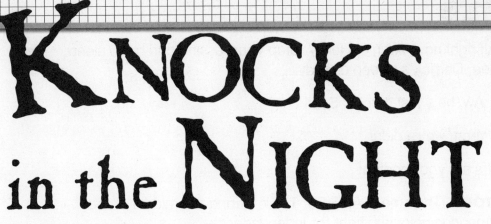

In 1777, the "Female Paul Revere" rides through a stormy night to warn the local militia of the advance of the British army.

CHARACTERS

SYBIL LUDINGTON (16 years)
ARCHIE LUDINGTON (10 years)
HENRY LUDINGTON, Jr. (8 years)
REBECCA LUDINGTON (14 years)
MARY LUDINGTON (12 years)
COLONEL HENRY LUDINGTON
MRS. ABIGAIL LUDINGTON
ZACH
MR. HIRAM POTTER
MRS. EMILY POTTER
MR. NORDSTROM
MAN 1
MAN 2
SOLDIER 1
SOLDIER 2
GENERAL GEORGE WASHINGTON
NARRATORS 1–8

1

SYBIL All right now, Archie, Henry. Stop your fussing and go to sleep. See, Derrick's asleep already.

ARCHIE Aw, he's just a baby, Sybil.

HENRY Yeah, we're older.

SYBIL It's still your bedtime.

NARRATOR 1 The time is April 26, 1777, during the middle of the American colonies' fight for independence.

NARRATOR 2 The place is Fredericksburg, New York.

NARRATOR 3 The scene is one that gets repeated every night in every household on the farms and in the villages and cities of this new land.

NARRATOR 4 But tonight will not be like every other night. Tonight Sybil Ludington will become a hero.

ARCHIE Can't we stay up just a little longer?

HENRY We haven't seen Pa for months, he's been off fighting.

SYBIL Henry, you were dozing off already, sitting by the fire. Pa's home now. You'll see him tomorrow.

ARCHIE Wait—listen. There's a horse. Somebody's come!

SYBIL Well, I'll go down and see who it is. But you two stay in bed.

SCENE 2

NARRATOR 5 The kitchen is a scene of some activity. There is a stranger at the door, and he looks like a wild man!

COLONEL LUDINGTON Come inside, quickly.

ZACH Thank you. You're Colonel Ludington?

COLONEL LUDINGTON I am. Here, sit down at the table. Abigail?

MRS. LUDINGTON Yes, Henry. Rebecca, Mary, get our guest some hot tea and biscuits and some of that ham.

REBECCA Yes, Ma.

ZACH I shouldn't. I'm all wet and muddy. It's raining pretty hard out there.

MRS. LUDINGTON Never mind that, it'll clean up. Sit, sit, and the girls'll bring you some food. You look exhausted.

ZACH Thank you, Mrs. Ludington. I've ridden over from Danbury.

REBECCA That's more than seventeen miles!

MARY In this kind of weather! You must be brave!

ZACH No, ma'am. But I've a message for the Colonel.

COLONEL LUDINGTON I knew it was too good to be true. I've just come home. My men are all on leave so they can do their spring planting.

ZACH Yes, sir. But things are bad. British soldiers have taken over Danbury.

MRS. LUDINGTON Oh, no!

REBECCA Here's some ham for you, and some fresh biscuits. We just made them tonight.

MARY And some nice, hot tea—with sugar!

ZACH Much obliged, ladies.

(Rebecca and Mary giggle together.)

COLONEL LUDINGTON What's your name, son?

ZACH Zach, sir.

COLONEL LUDINGTON Tell me, Zach.

ZACH Yes, sir. They come into town yesterday. Anchored in Long Island Sound, we think, and marched up through Reddings Ridge. Looks to be about two thousand of them, and we've only got about a hundred-fifty militia. Things are just out of control. Colonel, they're burning Danbury to the ground!

MRS. LUDINGTON That's where the Continental Army is storing all its supplies and ammunition, isn't it, Henry?

ZACH Yes, ma'am. They spared the church, and they marked crosses on the houses of folks loyal to the king. Those they spare, but then they're burning everything else.

NARRATOR 6 The messenger goes on to elaborate, details of what is burning.

NARRATOR 7 According to a later report, twenty-two stores and barns are destroyed this night, with all their contents.

NARRATOR 8 Nineteen private homes.

NARRATOR 1 And the Danbury Society Meeting House.

NARRATOR 2 Of the Continental Army supplies, four thousand barrels of beef and pork.

NARRATOR 3 One hundred barrels of biscuits.

NARRATOR 4 Eighty-nine barrels of rice.

NARRATOR 5 One hundred hogsheads of sugar and fifty of molasses.

NARRATOR 6 Twenty casks of coffee.

NARRATOR 7 Large stores of wheat, oats, and corn.

NARRATOR 8 Fifteen casks of medicines of all kinds.

NARRATOR 1 Over a thousand tents.

NARRATOR 2 Five thousand pairs of shoes and stockings.

NARRATOR 3 A large quantity of hospital bedding.

NARRATOR 4 Engineers' and carpenters' tools.

NARRATOR 5 And a complete printing press.

ZACH And I don't know how many of guns and ammunition, taken or destroyed.

MRS. LUDINGTON But Zach, what about the people?

ZACH Why, they're getting out, Mrs. Ludington, those that can. Hiding in the woods, a lot of them. Some folks taken prisoner.

REBECCA How awful for them!

ZACH Mostly they're just waiting and hoping for help to come.

MARY I hope those British don't come here!

COLONEL LUDINGTON Well, Mary, we'll just have to make sure they don't. *(To Zach.)* Who's in charge, do you know?

ZACH It's General Tyron.

COLONEL LUDINGTON William Tyron!

SYBIL You know him, don't you, Pa? Isn't he—?

COLONEL LUDINGTON He's the British-appointed Governor of New York. We served together. He's the one who appointed me captain in our colonial regiment before we formed the Continental Army to fight those British imperialists. It sickens me to think of him acting toward his own people like this.

ZACH Colonel Ludington, sir, your Seventh Regiment is the only colonial regiment between Danbury and Peekskill—

COLONEL LUDINGTON Yes, and we've got to get them back together. They won't be happy. They just got home. And it won't be easy. They're scattered all over the countryside.

MRS. LUDINGTON Henry, you got them together before, and you can do it again. You have to go rescue Danbury.

COLONEL LUDINGTON You're right. But how? I can't go. I've got to be here to get the men organized when they start to come in.

ZACH I'll go, sir. I'm feeling much better now I've had some food and a rest. Just you tell me where—Ahhh! *(He cries out in pain.)*

MRS. LUDINGTON Are you hurt?

ZACH No, ma'am. My horse shied at some branches and threw me, is all. It's nothing—

MRS. LUDINGTON Let me look at your ankle. Does that hurt?

ZACH Ahhh! No, ma'am, that doesn't hurt hardly at all.

COLONEL LUDINGTON Still, you're in no condition to get back on your horse for another long ride. But whom can I send?

ARCHIE We'll go, Pa! Me and Henry can ride together!

MRS. LUDINGTON Archie, Henry, what are you doing out of bed?

ARCHIE We heard that man ride up.

COLONEL LUDINGTON It's all right, Abigail. They deserve to know what's going on. But boys, you're just too young.

HENRY Awww, Pa!

SYBIL Pa, I can go. I'm sixteen now, and that's as old as a lot of boys gone for soldiers. And I can ride real well, you said so yourself. And Star knows me and likes me.

COLONEL LUDINGTON Yes, Sybil.

SYBIL After all, I practically raised her myself, and I've taken care of her—What?

COLONEL LUDINGTON I said yes. You are the one to go.

SYBIL Oh, thank you, Pa! I can do it, you'll see!

COLONEL LUDINGTON I'm sure you will. Archie, Henry, go out and saddle up Star for your sister.

ARCHIE All right, Pa.

COLONEL LUDINGTON And be sure you get that girth strap tight, you hear?

HENRY We will, Pa.

MRS. LUDINGTON Henry—

COLONEL LUDINGTON Abigail, I have no choice.

MRS. LUDINGTON You thought I was going to object to Sybil's going, but I'm not. You're right, she's the one to do it. Sybil, here—you'll need your warm wool cloak and your bonnet.

SYBIL Where do you want me to go, Pa?

COLONEL LUDINGTON Let's see. I think if you go south by the river, then along Hourse Pound Road to Mahopac [mah HOH pak] Pond. Then turn west and go to Red Mills, then north to Stormville. There'll be a lot of men scattered in farms off the road, but they'll start notifying each other. Tell them to muster here at dawn. And Sybil—

SYBIL Yes, Pa?

COLONEL LUDINGTON Be careful, my girl. Come back safe.

SYBIL I will, Pa.

SCENE 3

NARRATOR 6 As Sybil and her family leave the bright warmth of the kitchen for the chilly night darkness, they can see the sky glowing red.

REBECCA Look there, in the east. That's not lightning.

ZACH It's Danbury, burning.

MARY Oh, it must be an awful big fire!

ARCHIE Here's Star, Sybil. All saddled and ready for you.

SYBIL Thank you, Archie.

HENRY And here's a stick, in case you have to beat off any British soldiers.

SYBIL And thank you, Henry.

REBECCA Ohhh—you will be careful, won't you, Sybil? I'd just die if anything happened to you.

SYBIL I will, Rebecca.

MARY And when you come back, you'll tell us all about it—everything!

SYBIL I promise, Mary. Good-bye!

(The family members all ad lib their good-byes.)

MRS. LUDINGTON Henry, I know Sybil is a young woman now. She's sensible and responsible and all that, and I know she can do the job. But you won't think me awful if I worry about her—just a little bit?

COLONEL LUDINGTON Abigail, you can worry for both of us!

SCENE 4

NARRATOR 7 As Sybil Ludington starts off on her big night, the rain has let up a little bit, but there is more to come.

NARRATOR 8 The night is dark, except for that ominous red glow in the eastern sky, a constant reminder of the importance of her journey.

NARRATOR 1 And it is not an easy journey. There are many dangers.

NARRATOR 2 There are no paved roads. What roads there are are little more than wagon-wheel ruts.

NARRATOR 3 There are rocks to trip over, and holes to fall into.

NARRATOR 4 There are branches to duck.

NARRATOR 5 And mud—mud that makes it difficult for the horse, Star, to lift her feet.

NARRATOR 6 There are human dangers too. There are men called Cowboys, who are pro-British loyalists who steal for the British army. If they knew what she was doing, they'd try to stop her.

NARRATOR 7 And worse—the woods are full of men called Skinners, who are not really loyal to either the British or the American side but only to themselves, and who steal and kill at random.

NARRATOR 8 Sybil has lived here all her sixteen years, and she knows about all these dangers. Still, she faces them and rides on.

NARRATOR 1 Leaving her home, the mill that her father owns and runs in times of peace, she rides south by the river and on to the farmhouses along Horse Pound Road.

NARRATOR 2 They are all dark. It's a time all decent, hard-working people are in bed.

NARRATOR 3 But at least she knows the people who live there. Using the stick her brother Henry had given her, she pounds on the closed shutters.

SYBIL (*pounding with a stick*) Mr. Potter! Mr. Potter, wake up!

MRS. POTTER Hiram, listen. Somebody's knocking outside.

MR. POTTER What, at this time of night? Who is it? What do you want?

SYBIL It's me, Sybil Ludington, Mr. Potter. Pa sent me. The British are burning Danbury, and the Seventh Regiment has to muster at Ludington's Mill!

MRS. POTTER Merciful heavens! Hiram, you'd better get a-moving!

MR. POTTER I am, Emily, I am. You can get my gun down from over the fireplace—now, where are my pants?

NARRATOR 4 Sybil rides on. She repeats her message at farmhouse after farmhouse. On to Carmel, Mahopac, and Lake Mahopac. She doesn't know many people so far from home, but she can't afford to be shy.

SYBIL (*pounding with her stick*) The British are burning Danbury! All the Seventh Regiment muster at Ludington's Mill!

MR. NORDSTROM I'll be there. Tell me, did you see the Schuster brothers yet?

SYBIL No, I—I don't know them.

MR. NORDSTROM No, you wouldn't have. They live up that side road. You go on. I'll notify them.

SYBIL Thank you!

NARRATOR 5 On she rides, swinging west and then back north, heading for Stormville, north of Ludington's Mill.

NARRATOR 6 Somewhere along the road she hears rough voices in the dark. A curse and then a loud laugh.

NARRATOR 7 Are they soldiers? Or are they the dreaded Skinners, thieves and murders who live for themselves?

NARRATOR 8 Sybil takes no chances. She dismounts Star and leads her off the road where they stand under the trees as quietly as they can while two men pass in the other direction.

SYBIL (*whispering*) Easy, Star, shhh!

MAN 1 I told you there'd be nobody out tonight, not in this weather.

MAN 2 You can never tell. Maybe we'd get lucky.

MAN 1 Yeah, somebody with a purseful of gold, riding at night along this road!

MAN 2 Well—Oh blast! It's starting to rain again.

MAN 1 I tell you, I'm not staying out any longer. I'm heading home.

MAN 2 Yeah, me too.

NARRATOR 1 As they ride on by in the blackness of the rainy night, Sybil breathes a hugh sigh of relief. Then she climbs back up into the saddle again and urges Star onward.

NARRATOR 2 On she rides, now to Red Mills and Mahopac Mines. Knocking on doors throughout the night.

SYBIL (*pounding with her stick*) The British! Danbury's burning!

Knocks in the Night 9

NARRATOR 3 On she rides, to Kent Cliffs and Redding Corners.

SYBIL *(pounding)* All the men of the Seventh Regiment!

NARRATOR 4 On she rides, to Pecksville and up to Stormville.

SYBIL *(pounding)* Muster at Ludington's Mill!

SCENE 5

NARRATOR 5 When she finally nears her home again, it is nearly dawn.

NARRATOR 6 She has ridden in a big loop, some forty miles altogether.

NARRATOR 7 She is exhausted and filthy with mud, and her hand aches terribly from pounding with her stick on doors and shutters of every farmhouse and cabin she could find.

SYBIL Just a few more miles, Star. We're almost home now. You've been such a good, brave horse!

NARRATOR 8 And as she turns in the yard of Ludington's Mill—

SOLDIER 1 There she is—there's Sybil!

SOLDIER 2 Sybil! Well done, lass! There's a girl with real courage!

NARRATOR 1 There they are, some four hundred soldiers who have heeded her call and gathered together to reform their regiment.

NARRATOR 2 Four hundred soldiers grin at her in the dim, milky light just before dawn.

SOLDIER 1 Let's hear it for Sybil!

ALL AVAILABLE VOICES *(ad lib cheering)* Yay! Three cheers! Hurray for Sybil! She's the one!

SYBIL Hello, Pa.

COLONEL LUDINGTON There's my girl! You did it, Sybil! Look at the men, and more arriving every minute. We'll be ready to march on Danbury within the hour.

MRS. LUDINGTON Sybil, I'm so proud of you!

SYBIL Thanks, Ma.

ARCHIE Hey, good going, sis!

HENRY I told you she'd do the job, Archie. Just like a real soldier!

ARCHIE Well, Henry, I never said she wouldn't!

REBECCA Sybil, I am so glad you're home safe. Here, have some hot tea.

SYBIL Oh, thank you, Rebecca, I can use that!

REBECCA The soldiers are calling you a hero.

SYBIL I don't know about that.

REBECCA Well, that's what they say.

MARY Sybil, you promised to tell me everything that happened.

SYBIL Oh, and I will, Mary—but not right now. Right now what I need most is to go to bed.

MARY All right, but will you tell me one thing?

SYBIL Yes, if I can.

MARY Weren't you scared at all?

SYBIL Mary, there were moments—when I was terrified!

NARRATOR 3 But Sybil's story doesn't end there.

SCENE 6

NARRATOR 4 Some time later, after the fighting has run its course, and the British are gone from American shores, her father announces a visitor.

COLONEL LUDINGTON Sybil, there's somebody here who wants to meet you. He's ridden here from Philadelphia just to see you.

SYBIL Who is it, Pa?

COLONEL LUDINGTON May I present—General George Washington.

SYBIL Ohhh! General Washington!

GENERAL WASHINGTON How do you do, Miss Ludington. I've been hearing a great deal about you.

SYBIL Thank you, sir.

GENERAL WASHINGTON And I want to thank you in person, and to tell you something.

SYBIL Yes, sir?

GENERAL WASHINGTON Now that we've won the war, it's time to start building a new nation. We don't know how to do that, exactly. Nobody's ever done that before. But I do know one thing. A country with citizens like yourself—loyal patriots who put the welfare of others before their own comforts—such a country will be a great country!

NARRATOR 5 And that's the story of Sybil Ludington, the "female Paul Revere," who has proved that anyone, no matter how young, can do the right thing and make a difference.

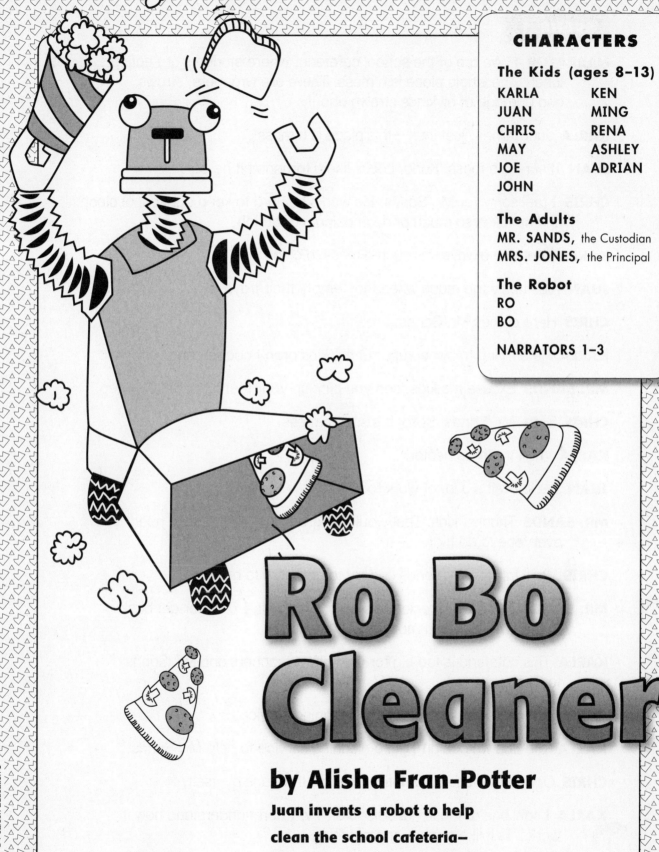

CHARACTERS

The Kids (ages 8–13)

KARLA	KEN
JUAN	MING
CHRIS	RENA
MAY	ASHLEY
JOE	ADRIAN
JOHN	

The Adults
MR. SANDS, the Custodian
MRS. JONES, the Principal

The Robot
RO
BO

NARRATORS 1–3

Ro Bo Cleaner

by Alisha Fran-Potter

Juan invents a robot to help
clean the school cafeteria—
then finds he needs to work
out some of the bugs.

SCENE 1

NARRATOR 1 We are at the school cafeteria, where students are eating lunch. The whole place is a mess. There are wrappers, straws, and garbage of all kinds strewn about.

KARLA Juan, Chris, just look—this place is a mess!

JUAN It sure is a mess, Karla. Looks like a tornado hit here!

CHRIS I feel sorry for Mr. Sands. He works so hard to keep our school clean, and he takes so much pride in doing a good job.

KARLA Yeah, he always has such a mess to clean up.

JUAN Kids hurry too much when they empty their trays.

CHRIS Here comes Mr. Sands.

KARLA He's trying to sweep up, but the kids aren't cooperating very well.

MR. SANDS Excuse me kids, can you pick up your feet? I need to sweep.

CHRIS Sure, Mr. Sands. Sorry it's such a mess.

KARLA We'll try to be neater.

JUAN We know it's a lot of work for you.

MR. SANDS Thanks, kids. That would be great. It's just that we need everyone to do that.

CHRIS We'll talk to our friends and try to get them to help too.

MR. SANDS I would appreciate that—thanks. Well, I'd better get back to the sweeping and mopping.

KARLA This cafeteria is too big for only a few teachers and Mr. Sands to clean up.

CHRIS It's not like he's our personal cleaning service.

KARLA Too bad we couldn't get a cleaning service to help Mr. Sands.

CHRIS Or one of those automatic vacuums that runs by itself.

KARLA I saw one of those advertised on TV. I don't understand how it works. Is it like a robot or something?

JUAN Karla, you just gave me a great idea! You and Chris come to my house after school today!

KARLA AND CHRIS Sure, Juan. What for?

JUAN You'll see after school!

CHRIS Hey, Juan, did you forget something?

KARLA Yeah, like your tray?

JUAN Oops, sorry about that. I'll dump it right now.

SCENE 2

NARRATOR 2 Karla and Chris show up at Juan's house after school that day, just as they promised.

KARLA So what is this brilliant idea, Juan?

CHRIS Yeah, I was wondering about it all afternoon.

JUAN Did you see that movie about robots last week?

CHRIS Was it on TV?

JUAN Yes. It was on cable.

KARLA I didn't see it. My mom doesn't let me watch much TV on weeknights.

JUAN Oh, it was awesome! This robot could walk and move just like people. It could talk and take instructions. And then they got to worrying whether it was developing an intelligence.

KARLA Cool!

JUAN Well, the scientist thought he'd better write some rules, so he started with "No robot may harm a human being," but the trouble was, he didn't think to program that in BEFORE he turned the robot on. . . .

CHRIS I think robots are kind of scary.

JUAN Not really, Chris. Robots are really just machines. It's how you USE them that's good or bad. But anyway, that movie gave me an idea. What if we had a robot that could help clean the cafeteria?

KARLA I think you've watched too much cable.

CHRIS What are you up to, Juan?

JUAN Just come with me. I'll give you a demonstration—downstairs in the basement.

CHRIS Looks creepy down there!

KARLA What is this place?

JUAN My father's workshop, Karla. He has some cool stuff down here.

CHRIS Wow! That looks like an old super vac. At home, my mom and dad just got a new one.

JUAN It is a super vac. I just added a few other things.

CHRIS Like, are these heating tubes?

KARLA Are they supposed to be arms and legs?

JUAN You got it!

CHRIS Cool! Are you going to show us how it works?

JUAN Yep. Just a minute—I have to make a mess for it to clean up.

CHRIS Here, I can dump out this trash can.

JUAN Great, just let me turn this on.

RO Sizzz . . . Sizzz . . . Sizzz . . . .

BO Errek . . . Errek . . . Errek . . . .

JUAN Watch it suck up all this junk.

RO Sizzz . . . Sizzz . . . Sizzz . . . .

BO Errek . . . Errek . . . Errek . . . .

KARLA It sure can clean!

JUAN And it even picks up spilt milk.

CHRIS That's great—'cause I seem to have butterfingers. I'm always spilling things.

JUAN Look, I made this sign for it. Read it.

KARLA I am Ro Bo Cleaner. Feed me. I eat with my feet.

CHRIS *(laughing)* That's great! I like it!

KARLA Me too, but how will it work in the cafeteria?

JUAN Easy, I just turn it on and it goes from table to table eating the trash.

CHRIS But how does it stop and go?

JUAN Oh. Well, I didn't think about that.

NARRATOR 3 Just then, the doorbell rings upstairs.

NARRATOR 1 Joe and May have also come to see what Juan is up to.

SCENE 3

MAY Hi Juan. We heard you had a big idea for the messy cafeteria.

JUAN Yeah, May, but we're just a little stuck at the moment.

JOE Maybe we can help.

MAY What are you working on?

KARLA Juan came up with this cool idea to make a robot he calls
Ro Bo Cleaner to eat the trash in the cafeteria.

MAY Wow, a robot cleaner? Well, let's see it.

JUAN Okay, it's in my basement. Follow me downstairs.

SCENE 4

MAY Is that it?

CHRIS Yes. That's it.

JOE Cool!

MAY How does it work?

JUAN Let me show you. I just have to make some more mess and plug
it in. Leave a little room in front of Ro Bo Cleaner, okay?

JOE I'll dump this garbage on the floor while you plug it in.

JUAN Okay, thanks. Here we go!

RO Slurp . . . Slurp . . . Slurp . . . .

BO Shoop . . . Shoop . . . Shoop . . . .

RO Vroom . . . Vroom . . . Vroom . . . .

BO Rev . . . Rev . . . Rev . . . .

JOE, MAY, CHRIS, and KARLA (*ad lib*) Hey, it works! Look at that!
I told you! Cool!

JOE That's terrific, Juan!

JUAN Thanks!

JOE So what's the problem?

KARLA We don't know how to get it to stop and go.

MAY I know! My brother has a remote control car he doesn't play with anymore. Maybe you could make a remote control for your Ro Bo Cleaner out of it.

CHRIS You mean like a vacuum with TV controls?

MAY Yes!

JUAN That's a great idea, May. You sure you can get the old remote?

MAY I'm pretty sure.

JUAN Thanks! I'll get Dad to help me hook it up. It'll be a piece of cake.

KARLA Wow! Problem-solving at its best. I'm sure glad we all got together today.

JUAN Thanks to you, Karla.

CHRIS My mom always says, "Two heads are better than one." Well, look how many heads we've got HERE!

SCENE 5

NARRATOR 2 A few days later the invention is ready.

JUAN I hooked up the robot with remote control buttons. It really works! I can make it go, stop, and turn.

JOE When can you bring it to school?

MAY I can't wait to see it.

KARLA Me too.

JUAN I'm going to bring it tomorrow.

CHRIS Let's tell Mrs. Jones about it.

SCENE 6

NARRATOR 3 The kids head for the office of Mrs. Jones, the principal.

MRS JONES So what can I do for you today? What's on your minds?

JUAN Mrs. Jones, we invented this vacuum we call Ro Bo Cleaner.

MAY It's to help Mr. Sands clean up the cafeteria.

MRS. JONES Ro Bo Cleaner? How does it work?

JOE Well, we hooked it to a remote control. Actually, Juan's Dad helped him hook it up.

KARLA They control it with a remote control. This way it moves from table to table to pick up all the trash in the cafeteria.

MRS. JONES Sounds interesting. I'm sure Mr. Sands will be excited to see this.

JUAN May we bring it to school tomorrow?

MRS. JONES Yes. Why don't you give us all a demonstration tomorrow during lunch?

JUAN We will! Thanks, Mrs. Jones.

SCENE 7

NARRATOR 1 The next morning Juan's father drives the Ro Bo Cleaner to school. Mrs. Jones keeps it in her office until lunchtime.

NARRATOR 2 At lunchtime Juan and Mrs. Jones roll the Ro Bo Cleaner into the cafeteria. They attract quite a crowd of curious students.

CHRIS Ta-daah!

KEN What is that?

MING It looks scary.

JOHN It looks like an alien!

RENA What does it do?

JUAN This is Ro Bo Cleaner!

KARLA It's going to help you clean up the cafeteria, Mr. Sands.

MR. SANDS It is? Well, this I have to see!

KEN Okay, but how?

MAY Juan has it hooked up to a remote control, so he can direct it.

MING It won't explode, will it?

JOE No, it's just to pick up the trash.

RENA Stop asking questions and let them show us!

NARRATOR 3 All the kids back away from Ro Bo Cleaner. They want to give it plenty of room to work.

JUAN Here's the plug. I'll just plug it into that wall socket over there . . . And I've got this LONG extension cord. . . .

KARLA At least this time you don't have to scatter any trash for Ro Bo to clean up.

CHRIS No, there's plenty of stuff on the cafeteria floor right now.

JUAN Now I'll start Ro Bo Cleaner from my remote. Here goes!

NARRATOR 1 And then Ro Bo Cleaner goes to work.

RO Sizzz . . . Sizzz . . . Sizzz . . . .

BO Errek . . . Errek . . . Errek . . . .

RO Slurp . . . Slurp . . . Slurp . . . .

BO Shoop . . . Shoop . . . Shoop . . . .

MING It's working!

JOHN This is great! Juan, you're a genius!

ALL KIDS Go Ro Bo! Go Ro Bo!

NARRATOR 2 In no time, all the straws, wrappers, and food spills are gone from the floor.

KEN Wow! What do you think, Mr. Sands?

MR. SANDS Well, kids, I must admit this contraption seems to be working just fine. But I hope it doesn't put me out of business.

NARRATOR 3 Juan works the controls and sends Ro Bo Cleaner to the next table, and the next, and the next.

NARRATOR 1 Just as at the first table, it cleans all the trash off the floor.

NARRATOR 2 Then it comes to the table where the twins are sitting, still eating their lunches.

RO Gulp . . . Gulp . . . Gulp.

BO Gulp . . . Gulp . . . Gulp.

ASHLEY My lunch! It's gone!

ADRIAN Mine too, Give it back!

JOHN The Ro Bo Cleaner took their lunches right out of their hands!

ASHLEY Make it stop! Make it stop!

JUAN I'm pushing every button I can!

ADRIAN Well, try some more!

KEN Here, let me try the controls . . . Oops, what went wrong?

RO Swish . . . Swish . . . Swish!

BO Spew . . . Spew . . . Spew!

ASHLEY Ro Bo Cleaner is starting to spit out everything it sucked up!

RENA It's spitting all over the walls and windows!

JOE And all over me! I feel sticky.

MING Whoa! What's this green goop? Pistachio pudding?

MAY Well that's better than creamed chicken. Ick!

RO Bleah . . . Bleah . . . Bleah!

BO Rwolf . . . Rwolf . . . Rwolf!

JOHN It's still out of control! Look!

ASHLEY *(screams)* Eeek! It has my hair!

ADRIAN Let go of my sister's hair!

RENA It won't stop!

JUAN Karla, pull the plug!

KARLA I've got it! There, it stopped!

MRS. JONES That's a relief!

MR. SANDS Kids, I know you meant well, but you ended up making my job bigger. Look at this mess!

JUAN I'm really sorry, Mr. Sands.

MRS. JONES I think Mr. Sands will forgive you if you help him clean up this mess. And you'd better do some more work on Ro Bo Cleaner. I don't think he—er, she—er, it?—is quite ready for prime time.

JUAN, CARLA, and CHRIS We will! Mr. Sands, where do we start?

Don't Judge a Book by Its Cover

by Maggie Gautier

CHARACTERS

Student Singers
MITA
ALISON
FRANK

Student Computer Experts
SOPHIE
ELLIOT
ROGER
MELODY
PETER

Howard School Faculty and Staff
MR. JOHNSON,
Bus Driver
MRS. O'LEARY,
Fifth-grade Teacher
MS. PEARLMAN,
Student Teacher

Hilltop Center Staff
MRS. SIMMS,
Activities Director
MRS. EDRAKI,
Facilities Manager
MR. ROLLEY,
Custodian

Hilltop Center Senior Citizens
MR. WASHINGTON
MR. ZIMMERMAN
MRS. SASSO
MRS. COSTER
MRS. TRUMPETER
MRS. JACKSON

NARRATORS 1–2

Computer-age kids learn they have a lot more in common with senior citizens than they realized.

MR. JOHNSON Walk, don't run! I don't want anybody to get hurt coming up the stairs before we even leave for the field trip.

MRS. O'LEARY Okay, Mr. Johnson. Looks like everybody's on board. Remember, put your seat belts on. I can see you. Elliot and Melody, buckle up.

ALL STUDENTS *(ad lib)* We are. We're ready. Let's go!

MR. JOHNSON And we're off.

MITA *(whispering to Sophie)* Gosh, Sophie, Mr. Johnson treats us like we're still in fourth grade. Why doesn't he just drive the bus and keep his comments to himself?

SOPHIE I know what you mean, Mita.

ELLIOT When I signed up to be a computer tutor, I thought I would be meeting some kids my own age, not a bunch of old people.

ROGER Right, Elliot. So how old are these people anyway? Fifty?

ELLIOT It's not fair. You tricked us, Mrs. O'Leary.

MRS. O'LEARY I did not trick you, Elliot, I promise. I thought you might like showing off how good you are on the computer to someone who may not know as much.

ELLIOT Yeah, but to an old person! What am I supposed to talk to them about?

MRS. O'LEARY Well for starters, you can talk to them about the computer. You'll be fine, I promise.

ELLIOT I don't see what's the big deal. My grandmother e-mails me all the time.

SOPHIE Mine too. I wish this bus were going to the animal shelter instead of an old people's home. It would be fun to play with the animals all afternoon.

ROGER I wish we were going to the ball game. That's a field trip worth taking!

MS. PEARLMAN Roger, did you know that if you get a great report card at the end of the year, the school gives out free tickets to a game for you and your family? It's a great deal.

MELODY I've heard about that, Ms. Pearlman. Do they really give out free tickets?

MS. PEARLMAN Sure they do, Melody. They've been doing it since I was in fifth grade.

PETER Wow. You went to school here. That was a long time ago, wasn't it?

MS. PEARLMAN It wasn't all THAT long ago! But I loved it here—that's why I wanted to come back now as a student teacher. You know, when I went to Howard School they didn't have the new gym built or the computer lab. But they were giving out tickets if you got good grades, so that part is the same.

MELODY Gee, I'm going to really hit the books when I get home!

ROGER I can just buy a ticket to the game.

MS. PEARLMAN Of course you can, but wouldn't you like to earn four tickets so you could take your family to the game?

ROGER I guess that would be pretty cool. But I've got a C in social studies.

MS. PEARLMAN Well, I'll ask Mrs. O'Leary if you can do an extra-credit project to boost your grade. It would also help if your assignments were on time.

ROGER I know. Will you help me with an extra-credit project?

MS. PEARLMAN I can help you, but I can't do it for you.

ELLIOT It's going to be weird talking about computers to a bunch of people who were born before computers were invented.

MS. PEARLMAN The good news is, they're interested, and that's what counts. If you're interested in something, you can usually do pretty well at it.

ELLIOT If you say so.

MRS. O'LEARY Listen, everybody! We'll be arriving at the Hilltop Senior Citizens Center in just a few minutes. I want to remind you for the last time to be on your best behavior. We're guests here, okay? Walk when you get off the bus, don't run.

ALL STUDENTS (ad lib) Yeah! We know! You told us a thousand times. Okay!

MRS. O'LEARY Put your nametags where everyone can see them, right above your hearts. Alison, Frank, and Mita, you'll be going to the music room with Ms. Pearlman. Everybody else will be going to the computer technology room with me.

ALISON Frank, I'm so nervous. It's scarier than singing in the school play.

FRANK Yeah. Did you bring your sheet music, Alison?

ALISON Right here. Did you bring yours?

FRANK It's in my backpack.

MELODY Well I'm a little nervous about this computer stuff. Is it just me?

PETER Yeah, Melody, it's just you.

MELODY Thanks a lot, Peter!

PETER No problem.

SCENE 2

NARRATOR 1 Meanwhile, the seniors at Hilltop Senior Citizens Center were getting ready to have visitors.

MRS. SIMMS The kids and their teachers are due any time. Now remember, this is a part of the fifth-grade community service program, so I want you to be on your best behavior. Try not to embarrass these nice kids.

MR. WASHINGTON What could we possibly do to embarrass them, Mrs. Simms?

MR. ZIMMERMAN Don't answer that! You don't want to give him any ideas.

MRS. SASSO Just don't sing, Mr. Washington. You'll embarrass me!

MR. WASHINGTON (singing loudly) When Irish Eyes are Smiling. . . .

ALL SENIORS (ad lib) Be quiet! Come on now! Please, not now!

MR. ZIMMERMAN Honestly, I'm not so sure this was a good idea. I don't even know how to type. If I leave now there won't be any harm done.

MRS. SASSO You can't leave now, Mr. Zimmerman. These kids have come a long way to help us, and besides, you've got nothing to be afraid of, computers or kids.

MR. ZIMMERMAN Afraid? What's there to be afraid of, Mrs. Sasso?

MRS. SASSO Oh, maybe being a beginner and not knowing how to do something. Don't you want to learn at least how to turn these things on?

MR. ZIMMERMAN Okay, you made your point. I'll stay.

MR. WASHINGTON Good, because if you left, I might be right behind you.

MRS. COSTER Well, gents, if you're staying—I guess I won't leave either.

MRS. TRUMPETER Hey, I'm really excited about all this. If I can figure out how to use this computer, I'm going to finally write my memoirs.

SCENE 3

NARRATOR 2 Just then, the fifth graders, Mrs. O'Leary, and Ms. Pearlman walked through the front door of the Center.

NARRATOR 1 Mrs. Edraki and Mrs. Simms from the Center were there to meet them.

MRS. EDRAKI Good afternoon, Mrs. O'Leary. It's nice to see you again.

MRS. O'LEARY Nice to see you too. I'd like you to meet Ms. Pearlman, our student teacher, and some of my students who have volunteered for today.

MRS. EDRAKI Hello everybody, I'm Mrs. Edraki, the Facilities Manager, and this is Mrs. Simms, the Activities Director. Thank you so much for coming.

ALL STUDENTS (ad lib) Hi. It's nice to meet you. Hello.

MRS. EDRAKI I know there are two groups here today; we have the singers and the computer experts. Mrs. Simms will be going with the singers to the music room, and I'll be going to the computer room with the tutors.

MS. PEARLMAN I'll be going with the musicians too. Mrs. Simms, I'd like you to meet Frank, Alison, and Mita. We've prepared some songs from the school play, where, I might add, they have lead roles.

MRS. SIMMS That's terrific. You'll be singing for members of the Hilltop Wholetones, our choir here. I imagine they'll teach you some of their songs.

MRS. EDRAKI The rest of you follow me. Just walk this way.

MRS. EDRAKI Here we are—the computer technology room. Fellow Hilltoppers, I'd like you to meet Mrs. O'Leary. She's the fifth-grade teacher from Howard School. And these kids are computer whizzes from her class.

MRS. O'LEARY Hello, everyone. I think some introductions are in order. Melody, why don't you start?

MELODY Hi. I'm Melody.

ALL SENIORS (*ad lib*) Hello, Melody.

NARRATOR 2 The introductions went around the room. Some of the seniors—and kids—were glad there were name tags to refer to, just in case.

MRS. EDRAKI Now that we've finished with the introductions, Mrs. O'Leary, I'm going to bow out. You and the kids take over, won't you?

MRS. O'LEARY Thank you, Mrs. Edraki. Let's start with basics, shall we? Elliot, why don't you turn this computer on and give us an overview?

ELLIOT Um, okay. First off, every computer is a little different. The main thing is to turn it on and just check it out. Sometimes the switch is on the back and sometimes the sides, but if you just look around you can find it. Here's the switch on this one. See, a light goes on when you turn it on.

MRS. TRUMPETER Is the keyboard just like a typewriter?

ROGER I think so, but it has a lot more keys. You use the keyboard to tell the computer what you want to do, and you use the mouse to move around the screen like I'm showing you now. The keyboard and the mouse work together as kind of a team.

MRS. O'LEARY Thanks, Elliot and Roger. Now Hilltop pupils, I'm going to assign each of you an individual tutor. But first, we'd like to hear from you. Tell us what you'd like to learn about the computer. Who wants to go first?

MR. WASHINGTON I will. I'm Mr. Washington. I need to learn about e-mail. You see, my son lives in Japan, and there's a twelve-hour time difference. I called him at 4:30 in the morning last week by mistake. I woke the whole family up, and that's when I promised I'd learn how to e-mail. He said I could get pictures of my grandkids really easily. Is that true?

© Pearson Education 5

ROGER Sure. It's easy. You use the scanner and the disk drive with the mouse.

MR. WASHINGTON Well, Roger, I think that's a bit over my head right now. . . . Hey, isn't that a Coyote shirt you're wearing?

ROGER Yeah, it's the new one. My Dad bought it for me at the game last week.

MR. WASHINGTON Good season this year, don't you think?

ROGER Great season. They may have a chance.

MR. WASHINGTON Well, when I coached them, it took us three years to get to the Nationals, but we finally got there. I've still got season tickets.

ROGER You coached the Coyotes? That's awesome!

MRS. O'LEARY I'll tell you what; when we finish the group session, Roger, why don't you be Mr. Washington's private tutor? Does that sound good?

ROGER AND MR. WASHINGTON *(ad lib)* Yeah. Sounds great.

MRS. O'LEARY Who's next?

MRS. COSTER Hi, boys and girls. I'm Mrs. Coster. My kids and grandkids keep telling me to adapt to new things. That's why I'm here.

MRS. O'LEARY Adapting is good, Mrs. Coster. It keeps our minds fresh. How about you—Mrs. Sasso?

MRS. SASSO Yes, that's me. I just I love going to the library, but carrying all those books home, even in a book bag, is so heavy. I read about a cooking school in Italy, and I want to see if maybe I can find out about it and if I can afford it.

SOPHIE Cooking schools in Italy? Do you want to become a chef?

MRS. SASSO No, honey. I love to cook, so I thought I'd combine two of my loves—travel and cooking.

ALL STUDENTS *(ad lib)* That's really cool! That would be a great class. Good idea!

MELODY You can do all kinds of research about other countries. When I was at camp, my Mom and Dad went on a tour of three countries in Europe. I helped them research it on the Web. They even bought their tickets on-line.

MRS. TRUMPETER What's the Web?

MELODY Oh, that's what they call it when you are looking for something using the Internet. They call it the World Wide Web.

PETER Do you want me to show you?

MRS. O'LEARY Peter, that's a great idea. But I think this is the perfect time for us to split up so that each person has a private tutor. It'll be easier to see and get some hands-on experience. Sophie, you work with Mrs. Sasso; Elliot, with Mr. Zimmerman; and Melody, with Mrs. Trumpeter. Roger, you and Mr. Washington work together. Peter, you'll be with Mrs. Coster.

NARRATOR 1 The fifth-grade tutors and the seniors paired up and began their private lessons.

MRS. TRUMPETER Well, Melony, I think I can get the hang of it. I already know how to type. I want to write my memoirs, you know.

MELODY Mrs. Trumpeter.

MRS. TRUMPETER Yes, Melony.

MELODY My name is Melody, like a song.

MRS. TRUMPETER I'm so sorry, honey. Here, let me put my glasses on. There it is, right there on your nametag. Melody, like a song—I'll remember that.

MELODY Thanks. So what's a memoir?

MRS. TRUMPETER It's the story about your life. I want to write it all down.

MR. ZIMMERMAN Well, Elliot, I know how to turn the thing on, but I haven't had much luck after that. I keep getting error messages, and I don't know what to do.

ELLIOT That's cool. I used to get them all the time. Let me show you this trick.

MR. ZIMMERMAN If I had to operate on your dog or give you the right medicine for a rattler bite, I could teach you how. But computers— you're the expert.

ELLIOT Did you ever get bitten by a snake?

MR. ZIMMERMAN Just once, a rattlesnake. When I was one of the vets at the zoo, I helped take care of all kinds of animals—monkeys, elephants, even snakes.

ELLIOT That would be awesome! We take our dog to the vet, but I never thought about being a zoo vet. Can anybody do it?

MR. ZIMMERMAN Sure, if you really want to. Tell you what, you look up career information about zoo vets on that Web thing—and I'll look up Peru. I've always wanted to go there.

ELLIOT Deal! Okay, let's get started. First, we dial up; then. . . .

NARRATOR 2 The minutes galloped by as the Hilltop seniors learned first-hand why kids are so crazy about computers.

MRS. COSTER Oh my!

MR. ZIMMERMAN Hey, what happened? The lights went out.

MRS. SASSO But look—the computers are still on.

NARRATOR 1 Before long, Mr. Rolley, the custodian, walked in carrying a big furry orange cat.

MR. ROLLEY Excuse me, Mrs. Edraki. It seems Chester here chewed through a wire in the basement, and that blew a fuse. It will only take a few minutes to fix. Say, I wonder if one of you kids could babysit Chester for me for a few minutes?

SOPHIE Oh yes, I'd love to, Mr. Rolley. Is it okay, Mrs. O'Leary?

MRS. O'LEARY I think so. Take him from Mr. Rolley—gently now. Yes, I think you and Chester will do just fine.

MRS. EDRAKI Well, it's a good time to take a break. I think we have cookies and juice in the kitchen. On the way there, we can take a quick tour of the building.

PETER Does anybody need to back up anything or save a document?

MRS. O'LEARY Good question, Peter. Why don't you all save your documents and turn the computers off? The kids will show you how.

SCENE 5

NARRATOR 2 The kids and the seniors followed Mrs. Edraki as she showed them around the center. Elliot walked beside Mr. Zimmerman, who was a real pro handling his electric wheelchair.

MR. ZIMMERMAN I can't climb mountains anymore, Elliot, but this thing sure helps me get around. My knees are bad, but they're not stopping me.

ELLIOT Oh. My grandfather uses a walker, but your wheelchair looks like more fun. Mr. Zimmerman, do people live here?

MR. ZIMMERMAN Yes, Eliot. Well, sort of. Some of us live in homes or apartments that are on the property. This building is the community center, and it's open to all seniors. We come here to take classes, play cards, talk politics, or just hang out.

MRS. SASSO Sometimes, we get together and go on bus trips to museums, to see a play, or to hear some music. You see, many of us don't drive any more.

MRS. TRUMPETER I hardly ever drove anyway, and the bus picks me up from home on the days that I come here. I do swim though. The pool here is so great with the glass roof. We can swim all year round.

MR. WASHINGTON When I retired, I drove my wife crazy sitting around the house all day. I found out about Hilltop, checked it out, and liked it right away.

MRS. EDRAKI Okay, everyone. We'll turn right here. This is the kitchen.

NARRATOR 1 The group rounded the corner. As Mrs. O'Leary turned into the kitchen, her face lit up.

MRS. O'LEARY Well, look who's here! Hi, Mom! I'd like you to meet some of my students. Everyone, this is my mother, Mrs. Jackson.

ALL STUDENTS *(ad lib)* Your Mom. Wow! It's her Mom.

MRS. JACKSON Hi, everybody. So you're the students I've been hearing all about. We've been having a ball singing with Allison, Frank, and Mita. I just stopped by to get some cookies for everyone in the choir room.

MRS. O'LEARY We're doing the same thing. Seems as if Chester chewed through some wires, and Mr. Rolley needed to fix a fuse. You know Chester, don't you, Mom? This is Sophie, holding him.

MRS. JACKSON Hello Sophie. Chester can be a real mischief-maker. It sure looks like you two have made friends.

SOPHIE Yes, Mrs. Jackson. I love cats. And Chester is so soft and adorable!

MRS. JACKSON I've got an idea. Why don't you all join us in the music room? We can all take a break together.

© Pearson Education 5

MRS. O'LEARY Great idea. Who wants to help carry the snacks?

ROGER and MELODY I will.

MRS. JACKSON It's this way down the hall. Just walk toward the music.

SCENE 6

NARRATOR 2 Mrs. Jackson, Mrs. O'Leary, and the kids entered the music room just as the singers were finishing up their last number.

MELODY Hi, everyone! Cookies and drinks are here!

NARRATOR 1 The kids and grownups made necessary introductions. They snacked and chatted. After a while, Mr. Rolley came in.

MR. ROLLEY Good news, everyone. The electricity is back on. You can go back to the computer room any time you want. Sophie, I'll take Chester back now.

MRS. O'LEARY Thanks, Mr. Rolley. Students, we don't have much time left. I think we'd better say our good-byes and go back to the computer room to get our things.

MRS. EDRAKI Yes, we understand. You have to get back to school on time. I think this has been a great opportunity. Did you computer pupils learn something today?

ALL SENIORS *(ad lib)* Yes. I sure did! Yeah, it was great!

MRS. O'LEARY That's terrific. I thought you'd be in good hands.

MRS. SIMMS Well, the Hilltop Wholetones were in top form today, so I'm guessing you singers had a good time—right?

ALL SENIORS *(ad lib)* You bet! What a treat! We made beautiful music together.

MITA Thanks, Mrs. Simms. Thanks everyone.

FRANK We really had fun!

ALISON We sure did!

MRS. JACKSON 'Bye now. It was so nice to meet all of you. Have a safe trip back.

SCENE 7

NARRATOR 2 Back in the computer room, the students gathered their book bags and belongings. Then they went to the front entrance to wait for Mr. Johnson and the bus. Everyone talked about the visit.

MS. PEARLMAN So you got to meet Mrs. O'Leary's mother. Do you think they look alike?

ALL STUDENTS (ad lib) Kind of. Not really. Yes. I think so. Maybe.

MRS. O'LEARY It seemed like everybody had a pretty good time. Are you looking forward to going back?

ROGER It wasn't all that bad. I thought Mr. Washington was pretty cool. He was a real coach for a real team. I got a few pointers.

MELODY It was kind of fun. I bet I can do some research for the next time.

ALLISON The singing was fun. The Wholetones were really good. And we knew some of the same songs.

FRANK You know, my mom likes to say, "Don't judge a book by its cover." I kept thinking about that. People here look old, and some of them can't get around very well. But inside, I think they're just like us. They want to make friends. They want to learn new things and have a good time.

MS. PEARLMAN Frank, I think your mom is very wise. And—so are you!

MRS. O'LEARY Well students, do you want to come back in two weeks? You don't have to make up your minds right now. You can think about it.

ALL STUDENTS (ad lib) Oh yeah! We want to come back! Sure!

MRS. O'LEARY Wonderful. It's a deal.

NARRATOR 1 Just then, Mr. Johnson came in the front door.

MR. JOHNSON Okay, kids. I've pulled the bus up front. It's time to load up. Walk, don't run. I don't want to be responsible for any injuries!

MITA and SOPHIE Here we go again!

Adventure by the Barrel

by Peter Grahame

Some folks just can't resist a challenge ... no matter how big, how loud, or how wet!

CHARACTERS

ANNIE TAYLOR
P. T. BARNUM
BARREL BUILDER
FRANK RUSSELL
FRED TRUESDALE
TOM BRADY
BOBBY LEACH
JEAN FRANCOIS BLONDIN
HARRY, Blondin's friend
JEAN LUSSIER
MR. WOODWARD
ROGER WOODWARD (7 years)
CAPTAIN, Maid of the Mist
NARRATORS 1–8
AUDIENCE MEMBERS 1–2
REPORTERS 1–3
ONLOOKERS 1–4
PASSENGERS 1–2
SOUND EFFECTS

NARRATOR 1 Welcome to Adventure Theater!

SOUND EFFECTS *(tooting like a trumpet)* Ta ta ta TAH ta TAH!

NARRATOR 2 Coming to you LIVE, right now, from your imagination!

NARRATOR 3 Today we're off to Niagara Falls.

NARRATOR 4 Upstate New York.

NARRATOR 5 At the border of America and Canada.

NARRATOR 6 A fantastic natural wonder!

NARRATOR 7 Hundreds of tons of water falling hundreds of feet over the edge.

NARRATOR 8 Every minute!

ALL AVAILABLE VOICES *(ad lib)* Wow!

NARRATOR 1 What power!

NARRATOR 2 What majesty!

NARRATOR 3 Millions of people come from all over the world just to see it.

NARRATOR 4 But wait. Some have experienced the falls in very unusual ways.

NARRATOR 5 Would you believe it? A few daredevils have ridden over the falls in barrels or huge, bouncing balls.

AUDIENCE MEMBER 1 What!? Why, that's crazy!

NARRATOR 6 How about an acrobat walking on a tightrope stretched over the falls?

AUDIENCE MEMBER 2 No . . . surely not!

NARRATOR 7 Believe it or not, some people actually tried these dangerous stunts—and succeeded.

AUDIENCE MEMBER 1 Well, I can't imagine ANYONE in their right mind climbing into a barrel and heading for that watery plunge!

NARRATOR 8 Annie Taylor did. And by all accounts, she WAS in her right mind.

NARRATOR 1 Annie was the first person ever to go over Niagara Falls in a barrel. But let's ask her to tell her own story. Mrs. Taylor, why DID you decide to take on Niagara Falls?

SCENE 2

TAYLOR Well, to tell the truth, I did it for the money. See, there was this famous circus owner named P. T. Barnum . . .

P. T. BARNUM *(very grandly)* I, P. T. Barnum, master of the GREATEST circus on earth, will give a big reward to the first person to go over Niagara Falls in a barrel!

TAYLOR Good old P. T.! He loved stunts like that. Well, as I said, I needed money at the time, so I thought, why not? Anyway, my mother used to say, "Annie, you're a daredevil at heart." I guess that tells you something. *(Pause.)* Now, if you're going to tackle Niagara Falls, you'd better have a good strong barrel. So my next step was to visit a barrel maker.

BARREL BUILDER No! No! I'll not make such a barrel for you! It's a crazy idea!

TAYLOR Look, I've got the plans all drawn up. And I came to you because you're the best cooper there is. If you don't help me, I'll just go somewhere else.

BARREL BUILDER Wait! You're right. I am the best. If you're going to do this, then the barrel must be very well built. By me. I'll do it.

TAYLOR Oh, thank you!

BARREL BUILDER But I still think it's a crazy idea, Mrs. Taylor!

NARRATOR 2 Annie didn't wait around to hear any more opinions from the barrel builder. She had a lot of other business to attend to.

TAYLOR Now I need to find a manager—someone to take care of details.

RUSSELL That's me, Frank Russell. After you do this, people will pay to hear you talk about it, Mrs. Taylor.

TAYLOR You may call me Annie.

RUSSELL Thank you. And please call me Frank.

TAYLOR Now we'll need somebody to tow the barrel out into the river above the falls.

RUSSELL Let me introduce Fred Truesdale, Annie. He's the one for the job.

TRUESDALE Call me Fred. I'm known as an expert river captain in these parts.

NARRATOR 3 Not everybody believed that Annie would really go over the falls.

NARRATOR 4 Several times she had to postpone the stunt.

REPORTER 1 Hey, Russell. I'm a reporter. Is Annie Taylor going to go over the falls in a barrel or NOT?

RUSSELL She will, she will.

REPORTER 2 Well, where is she today? And where was she yesterday?

RUSSELL Look, the weather has been bad.

REPORTER 3 Ha! I think this whole thing is a hoax. That's what I'm going to write in my column.

NARRATOR 5 But it wasn't a hoax. At one-thirty in the afternoon, on Thursday, October 24, 1901 . . .

TAYLOR I'm ready to do it. Let's go.

NARRATOR 6 Annie got into the barrel and buckled herself into a special harness.

NARRATOR 7 There were two cushions and a pillow in there, too.

NARRATOR 8 They set the barrel in the water, towed it out to the middle of the stream, and headed straight for the falls.

TAYLOR *(muffled)* Oh, Fred?

TRUESDALE *(loudly)* What is it?

TAYLOR *(muffled)* The barrel is leaking!

TRUESDALE It is? How much water is in there?

TAYLOR *(muffled)* About a bucketful.

TRUESDALE That won't hurt you. You'll be up and over, and we'll have you out in no time. Don't you worry.

TAYLOR *(muffled)* Okay. Goodbye . . .

NARRATOR 1 There was a big crowd of people watching as the barrel drifted faster and faster toward the edge of the falls.

NARRATOR 2 What was Annie feeling inside? Imagine being inside that barrel yourself.

NARRATOR 3 What would YOU feel? Would you be afraid? Or would you be having the time of your life?

NARRATOR 4 Hey, Annie, what's it like in there?

TAYLOR *(muffled)* I can feel the barrel gliding along kind of bumpy-like. Whoops! Now I'm turning around and around really fast, like on a ride at the amusement park. Oh there, that's over. Now I'm just floating along as nice as you please. You know, this isn't so bad, in fact . . .

ALL ONLOOKERS *(very anxious, building suspense)* Closer, closer, oh-h-h-h!

TAYLOR *(muffled)* I kind of like this. Why, I'll bet that when I reach the edge, it's just like . . .

ALL ONLOOKERS Closer, closer! And over she goes!

TAYLOR *(muffled)* Fly-y-y-y-ing!!! Oh!

SOUND EFFECTS *(water sound)* Aaaaahhhhhh! Ker-plosh!

NARRATOR 5 The barrel sank, then came up, then it bounced under the falls again, and finally it landed on the rocks.

TRUESDALE There it is, there it is! Somebody help me get it to shore!

BRADY Name's Tom Brady. Hang on. I'll just reach down and grab that rope on the barrel head. Then you help me pull it up!

TRUESDALE and BRADY *(ad lib)* Uh! Uh! Lift! Pull harder! Hurry! Uh! Uh!

NARRATOR 6 At last the barrel was on shore.

TRUESDALE Open it up, quick! Is she all right?

TAYLOR *(tired and weak)* Yes, Fred, I'm . . . I'm all right.

NARRATOR 7 The newspaper reporters pushed forward.

REPORTER 1 Annie Taylor, you did it!

REPORTER 2 You went over Niagara Falls in a barrel!

REPORTER 3 Well, Mrs. Taylor, what have you got to say for yourself?

TAYLOR No one should ever do that again. I certainly won't.

NARRATOR 8 Annie Taylor's story is well known today. But back then, she didn't become nearly as famous or as rich as she had hoped.

NARRATOR 1 And although Annie had said that "no one should ever do that again," many others did try it.

NARRATOR 2 In fact, the very next person to take on the falls was the one who became famous for it!

TAYLOR Wouldn't you know? And why did that person become famous for doing what I had already done?

NARRATOR 3 His name was Bobby Leach.

TAYLOR Because he was a man, that's why! Why, of all the nerve . . . !

LEACH Hel-lo, everybody! Bobby Leach is the name, Bobby "Big Time" Leach! Step aside, step aside. I'm going to go over Niagara Falls in a barrel!

NARRATOR 4 He was big time, all right. Big and loud. Fast talking.

NARRATOR 5 Always telling jokes.

NARRATOR 6 And the reporters really liked him.

REPORTER 1 Hey, Bobby! Over here! Tell us all about it!

REPORTER 2 Are you really going over the falls in a barrel?

LEACH That's right!

REPORTER 3 Wow, Bobby, you'll be the first man to ever do it!

TAYLOR What!? The first . . . why of all the . . . I, Annie Taylor, was first!

LEACH Yes, I'm going to make history, folks! Step aside, step aside!

NARRATOR 7 And on July 25, 1911, Bobby did it.

NARRATOR 8 Only his barrel was made of steel, not wood like Annie's barrel.

NARRATOR 1 What's more, they made a movie of it.

NARRATOR 2 And Bobby Leach became a big celebrity.

ONLOOKERS 1–4 *(ad lib)* Hooray for Bobby! Hooray for Bobby!

TAYLOR Well, isn't that a big load of baloney!

NARRATOR 3 But today, Annie Taylor is still remembered as the first person to go over Niagara Falls in a barrel.

TAYLOR Thank goodness for that!

SCENE 4

NARRATOR 4 Yes, you were the first, Annie, to go OVER the falls. But even before you, there was a French circus performer named Jean Francois Blondin (ZHAWN   frahn SWAH   blwan DAN).

TAYLOR Oh, I knew about him.

BLONDIN Move over, Annie; it's my turn. *(Pause.)* Greetings all, I'm Blondin the Magnificent!

NARRATOR 5 Blondin walked on a tightrope stretched across the Falls!

BLONDIN But I did much more than merely WALK across!

NARRATOR 6 Let's go back in time to June 30, 1859. Blondin's assistants have carefully strung the tightrope from side to side above the falls. Jean tests the rope with one toe, then starts across.

ONLOOKER 1 There he is!

ONLOOKER 2 Where?

ONLOOKER 1 Way up there, in the middle!

ONLOOKER 3 He stopped! What's he doing?

ONLOOKER 4 He's lowering a rope all the way down to that boat—now it looks like he's pulling up a bottle of water!

ONLOOKER 3 My oh my, he's sitting right down on the rope . . .

ONLOOKER 1 And he's having a drink of water!

ONLOOKER 2 There, he's up again—he has his balancing pole—now he's stopped again. What's he going to do?

ALL AVAILABLE VOICES *(gasping, ad lib)* Ah! Wow!

ONLOOKER 4 He just did a backward somersault!

ONLOOKER 2 Now he's walking again.

ONLOOKER 3 He's made it to the other side!

BLONDIN You haven't seen anything, folks. I'm going to do it again!

NARRATOR 7 The next time he went across . . .

ONLOOKER 1 On a bicycle!

NARRATOR 8 Then he did it . . .

ONLOOKER 2 Blindfolded!

NARRATOR 1 And what did he do for his last trip across?

BLONDIN I carried my friend Harry across on my back! *(Pause.)* Here we go, Harry. Hold on. We'll make it.

HARRY Blondin! The rope is swaying back and forth—a lot!

BLONDIN Let's just make it to the next section—uh—there! I have to rest, Harry, so get down.

HARRY Get down!?!

BLONDIN Don't worry, I'll hold you. Just for a minute.

NARRATOR 2 Then he picked poor Harry up again, and went on.

BLONDIN We'll make it to the next section and—whoops! The rope is really swaying again! Hold on, Harry, hold on!

HARRY I'm holding, I'm holding!

NARRATOR 3 Finally, after several near mishaps, they made it to the other shore.

ALL AVAILABLE VOICES *(ad lib)* Hooray! Hooray! They did it! What a sight!

REPORTER 1 You certainly were brave, you two!

REPORTER 2 For our newspaper readers, Blondin, tell us, were you scared?

BLONDIN *(loudly, to all)* What? Scared!? Me? Scared! Ha! No, I wasn't scared! *(Quietly, aside.)* I was terrified. *(To all.)* But we made it! Me and Harry! Harry? Harry? Where are you?

REPORTER 1 Uh, I think he's fainted.

BLONDIN Oh.

NARRATOR 4 Over the years, there were many people who attempted these amazing stunts.

NARRATOR 5 Like Jean Lussier (JEEN loo SEER).

LUSSIER That's me. I was a circus stuntman and a racing car driver, and I went over the falls in an eight-foot orange rubber ball. It had a steel frame, and it was lined with thirty-two inner tubes. I made it myself!

NARRATOR 6 And on July 4, 1928, Lussier went over.

SOUND EFFECT (a bouncing sound) Boing! Boing! Boing!

ONLOOKER 1 It's bouncing like a toy ball!

ONLOOKER 2 Now it's going straight down!

ONLOOKER 3 There! Now they're pulling it out of the water!

ONLOOKER 4 Is he . . . is he . . . safe?

ONLOOKERS 1–4 (ad lib) He made it! Hooray! Hooray!

LUSSIER I sure did. And after it was all over, I cut up the inner tubes and sold the pieces as souvenirs. Never did make much money, though. Still, it was a great trip! And I told my story over and over . . .

ONLOOKERS 1–4 (bored) And over and over and over . . .

NARRATOR 7 Enough already! There are other stories to tell.

NARRATOR 8 And perhaps there is no story quite so amazing as Roger Woodward's story.

NARRATOR 1 He went over the falls, but not on purpose.

NARRATOR 2 It was an accident.

NARRATOR 3 And he didn't even have a barrel!

ROGER I sure didn't.

NARRATOR 4 And he was only seven years old!

NARRATOR 5 The day was July 9, 1960. Roger and his older sister Deanne went for a boat ride with a friend. As the boat moved away, Roger's Dad called to him . . .

MR. WOODWARD Don't forget to wear your life jacket, son!

ROGER I won't, Dad! I'll put it on right now—I promise!

NARRATOR 6 No one ever understood how the boat was allowed to get so near the falls. But it did. And then something happened.

NARRATOR 7 The propeller hit a snag in the water and the boat motor stopped.

ROGER The motor's off! We can't get it started! And there's a big wave coming right at us! Help!

NARRATOR 8 All three passengers were thrown into the water.

NARRATOR 1 At first Roger was very frightened.

ROGER Ouch! Those rocks are hurting me!

NARRATOR 2 Then he saw people on land.

NARRATOR 3 And he got angry.

ROGER Why are those people just running along the shore? Why don't they come in and get me?

NARRATOR 4 You see, Roger still didn't realize that he was headed straight for the edge of the falls. No one could get in to save him.

NARRATOR 5 Then, suddenly, Roger did realize what was going to happen. And instead of being terrified, he felt very peaceful.

ROGER Gee. I guess I'm going over. I hope Mom and Dad will take care of my dog, Fritzy. Oh! Oh-h-h-h!

NARRATOR 6 Yes, poor Roger went right over the falls, wearing only a life jacket over his bathing suit.

NARRATOR 7 Far down below was the famous touring boat called the *Maid of the Mist*. The Captain looked out over the bow.

CAPTAIN I'm getting a bit too close to the falls with my tour group here. I'd better turn back now. Say, what is that passenger shouting about?

PASSENGER 1 Help! Quick! Someone is in the water!

CAPTAIN I see him! There, in the red life jacket! Throw out a life preserver! I'll swing the boat around so we can get him.

NARRATOR 8 Roger flung himself on the life preserver, tied to a long rope, and they hauled him toward the boat.

CAPTAIN What is that kid yelling?

ROGER (calling) My sister! Where is Deanne?

NARRATOR 1 Although Roger had just been the first person in history to survive the falls without the protection of a barrel or giant ball, he could think only of his sister's safety at that moment.

NARRATOR 2 In fact, Deanne was okay. Two brave people had jumped in the river and pulled her to safety before she reached the falls.

NARRATOR 3 When Roger was safely on the *Maid of the Mist*, he looked up at all the anxious faces around him.

ROGER Could I have a glass of water, please?

PASSENGER 2 Water? You want water?

PASSENGER 1 After all you had to drink?

ROGER The river tasted funny.

ALL AVAILABLE VOICES (ad lib) Well, I'll be. Can you beat that? He wants water! (All laugh, relieved.)

SCENE 7

NARRATOR 4 Since the mid 1800s, there have been many people who have tried to go over the falls.

NARRATOR 5 They went over in all kinds of barrels, or large balls, or other odd devices.

NARRATOR 6 They tried to walk over, jump over, or ride over in a small boat!

NARRATOR 7 Some of them made it. But many did not.

NARRATOR 8 But why? Why did they do it?

TAYLOR Well, for money, and a little fame. I was the first, the VERY first . . . but that big-time operator Bobby Leach . . .

LEACH I got lots of money and lots of fame. Ha, ha! How about you, Lussier?

LUSSIER I did it so I could tell a good story. Blondin? What about you?

BLONDIN I walked over on a tightrope because . . . well, because I could! And how about you, Roger?

ROGER I didn't want to go at all!

ALL AVAILABLE VOICES *(laughing, ad lib)* That's right! You sure didn't!

NARRATOR 1 Were they silly? Or were they heroes? What do you think? Would you like to go over Niagara Falls in a barrel?

NARRATOR 2 Well, there are very good reasons why you shouldn't.

NARRATOR 3 First of all, it's very dangerous. For every lucky survivor, there are other daredevils who never returned from their plunge.

NARRATOR 4 Not only that, it's against the law!

NARRATOR 5 So if you really want to tackle Niagara Falls . . .

NARRATOR 6 Use your imagination!

NARRATOR 7 It's a lot wiser.

NARRATOR 8 And a lot safer!

SUBURBAN POWER!

by Cynthia Gallaher

A power blackout disrupts routines but pulls neighbors together in an evening of fun, sharing, and conversation.

CHARACTERS

MRS. JANE COURTNEY
MR. BILL COURTNEY
JESSICA COURTNEY (13 years)
TYLER COURTNEY (11 years)
WILL COURTNEY (9 years)
MRS. SUE NOVAK
MR. JOE NOVAK
AMANDA (12 years)
BAE (12 years)
JUNG (10 years)
MR. TITO PEREZ
MR. DIEGO PEREZ
NARRATORS 1–4

MRS. COURTNEY (calling) Jessica, where are you?

JESSICA Upstairs, Mom. I'm in California.

MRS. COURTNEY California?

JESSICA I'm in the California Surfer Chat Room talking with a girl my age.

MRS. COURTNEY (to herself) Lots of surfing going on here in the Detroit suburbs. (Calling.) What about girls your age from school?

JESSICA They live on the other side of town. Anyway, they're not into surfing.

MRS. COURTNEY I wonder why.

NARRATOR 1 Mr. Courtney picks up on Mrs. Courtney's idea. He's just come back from an errand outside in the bright afternoon sun.

MR. COURTNEY Tyler, how about going outside? It's a beautiful Saturday.

TYLER But no one else is out. Anyway, I'm on the Internet with a boy from Japan.

MR. COURTNEY He speaks English?

TYLER Dad, videogames are the international language.

MR. COURTNEY So how about getting together with those new Korean boys across the yard from us?

TYLER But do they speak English?

MR. COURTNEY Aargh!

MRS. COURTNEY Will, all three of you kids need to go outdoors!

WILL I'm watching a mystery on DVD, Mom. The STORY's happening outdoors—they're skiing in the Swiss Alps.

MR. COURTNEY Will, when I was a kid in Detroit, I climbed trees.

MRS. COURTNEY And I jumped rope.

WILL But the suburbs are different. There's nothing to do. And anything that's happening around here can't be as fun as computers or DVDs.

MRS. COURTNEY California? Japan? Mysteries! Is anything real in the suburbs anymore?

MR. COURTNEY Huh? What was that sound?

WILL The TV shut off! It just went completely dark.

MRS. COURTNEY And the clothes dryer stopped.

MR. COURTNEY The power's out. Is that real enough for you, honey?

MRS. COURTNEY Very funny!

NARRATOR 2 Jessica runs downstairs breathlessly.

JESSICA Hey, my computer just died!

TYLER And yours doesn't work anymore either, Dad.

MR. COURTNEY The power's gone out. There's no electricity.

JESSICA The house is so quiet. Can't you hear it?

WILL How can you hear quiet?

TYLER All I know is, it's starting to get warm in here.

MRS. COURTNEY The air conditioning's out, too.

TYLER There's an old box fan in the closet we could use.

JESSICA That takes electricity too, silly.

MRS. COURTNEY Did someone say quiet? I can hear Dad's stomach growl.

MR. COURTNEY You know my stomach well. It's programmed to start thinking about supper right about now.

MRS. COURTNEY Do frozen steaks sound appetizing?

JESSICA Dad, maybe it's a good time to start that diet.

MR. COURTNEY Cute! Let's take those steaks out now. By grilling time, I'll bet they'll be thawed enough. Thank goodness we have a gas grill on the patio.

WILL Maybe we're not the only house without electricity.

TYLER Who's going to find out?

WILL I'm taking this pair of binoculars to scout the neighborhood for clues.

MRS. COURTNEY And while you're at it, I have another caper for you to solve.

WILL What do you mean?

MRS. COURTNEY Try to find a couple of ancient and mysterious items—a clothesline and some clothes pins.

WILL What are those?

MRS. COURTNEY If you're a good detective, you'll find out.

JESSICA It's getting hot in here now! First, I'm putting on my swimsuit. Then I'm going outside, shutting my eyes, and pretending I'm on a California beach.

TYLER Maybe I can use this softball and bat Uncle Walter gave me for my birthday a couple of years ago. They're a little dusty.

MRS. COURTNEY Good. Go out and see if you can knock some cobwebs off.

SCENE 2

NARRATOR 3 Mr. and Mrs. Courtney and Will head outside. Will sets off down the block to scout out what's happening. Mr. Courtney takes the cover off the patio grill. Mrs. Courtney moves a hamper of wet laundry outside and sits down at the picnic table.

NARRATOR 4 Just then, their next-door neighbor, Mrs. Novak, steps down her back steps holding a tray with a large pitcher and some glasses.

MRS. NOVAK How about some lemonade, neighbors? Don't know how long we'll need to cool off until the power's back on.

MRS. COURTNEY Thanks, Sue. Come sit on the patio with me. Let's have happy hour.

MRS. NOVAK Nothing beats visiting face to face for a change.

MRS. COURTNEY Right! I mean, we've phoned and e-mailed, but when was the last time we actually sat down and chatted?

MRS. NOVAK Let's make up for that right now!

NARRATOR 1 Jessica finally emerges from the house.

JESSICA Oh hi, Mrs. Novak.

MRS. NOVAK Hi Jessica, honey. Sit down and have some lemonade with us.

NARRATOR 2 But just then, Jessica notices a girl in the yard on the other side of theirs. She's wearing a tutu, doing ballet steps.

JESSICA No thanks, Mrs. Novak. I think I'll pop over next door and introduce myself to—well, to that girl.

NARRATOR 3 Though the new neighbors on the east side of the Courtneys moved in nearly four months ago, Jessica hasn't gotten to know Amanda, since they go to different schools.

JESSICA Hi. I'm Jessica.

AMANDA Hi. My name's Amanda.

JESSICA Do you like to surf?

AMANDA Who surfs around here?

JESSICA Someday I'm going to California. But I already know how to stand on a surfboard.

AMANDA Pretend that plank my dad left on the ground is a surfboard.

JESSICA It's easy, like this. You place one foot on the front right and the other on the back left and just hang your toes off the edges. Then just bend your knees. . . . Say, do you mind if I ask? Why are you wearing that funny dress?

AMANDA I take ballet. This is called a tutu. It's a costume ballet dancers wear.

JESSICA Cool. Show me something you can do, okay?

AMANDA Sure!

NARRATOR 4 Meanwhile, Tyler, holding bat and ball, sees the two Korean brothers out in their yard and goes up to them.

TYLER I know I never talked with you guys before, but my name's Tyler.

BAE Hi, I'm Bae (BAY).

JUNG I'm Jung. Hi.

TYLER Hi. And you probably haven't ever seen a bat and ball before.

JUNG Of course we have. Why wouldn't we?

TYLER Wow. You sure speak English well.

BAE We were born in Chicago.

TYLER You were?

JUNG And we played softball there too.

BAE And here.

JUNG So how's your pitching?

TYLER I'm a little dusty. I mean rusty.

JUNG We'll take care of you.

BAE and JUNG Hana, dul, set. . . One, two, three.

TYLER So you speak Korean, after all.

BAE Our parents speak Korean, so we speak Korean.

JUNG Don't your parents speak English?

TYLER Sometimes I think they speak a language from outer space.

SCENE 3

MRS. COURTNEY Oh, there's Will. Hi, Will. What have you got there?

WILL Clothesline and clothespins, Mom. The older lady in that green house across the street was hanging her clothes to dry and she had extras.

MRS. COURTNEY Thanks, Will. That's Mrs. Hurley, I believe. Did you thank her?

WILL Yes, Mom, I did. Really!

MRS. NOVAK Look, Jane, these clothespins are antiques! You could take them on one of those TV shows where they tell you how valuable your old things are.

MRS. COURTNEY Sue, you and I are spoiled by our electric dryers. I remember my own mom having clothespins like that—when I was a little girl.

MRS NOVAK Well, let me help you hang up your clothes.

MRS. COURTNEY Thanks, Sue. We can string this clothesline up between the house and that tree. It'll only take a minute. Then we can get back to important business.

MRS. NOVAK You mean happy hour?

MRS. COURTNEY Right you are! (*Mrs. Courtney and Mrs. Novak laugh.*)

WILL Mom? Is it okay if I walk down to the library? I want to see what's going on with the power in the rest of our neighborhood.

MRS. COURTNEY Sure. Be careful crossing streets.

SCENE 4

TYLER Dad, can we move the sprinklers from the back yard? We want to have a softball game.

MR. COURTNEY Sure, Tyler. Hi, boys.

JUNG and BAE Hi, Mr. Courtney.

MR. COURTNEY Come on. Let's move those sprinklers.

JESSICA Hey, guys!

AMANDA Can we play softball, too?

TYLER Are you girls good outfielders? Because there are a couple of trees out there where we keep hitting balls.

BAE If you would climb those trees, you could catch the balls while you balance on the tree limbs.

JESSICA Ha, ha! Very funny!

AMANDA But hey—we can handle outfielding. Right, Jessica?

JESSICA Right, Amanda!

AMANDA and JESSICA We're in!

MR. COURTNEY I'll turn on the gas on the grill, now, honey. The steaks look thawed.

MRS. COURTNEY That sounds fine. But what will we have WITH the steaks?

MRS. NOVAK We can have a big salad. I've got three heads of lettuce in my refrigerator that will spoil unless I go ahead and use them. And Joe has a great crop of tomatoes on his tomato plants. I'll go get the lettuce and find Joe.

MRS. COURTNEY Sounds wonderful, Sue. I'm sure I have some bread, butter, and garlic. We'll make some garlic toast on the grill, too.

MR. COURTNEY And I'll get the card table and set it up next to the picnic table.

MRS. NOVAK We're throwing a potluck! What fun!

NARRATOR 1 Before long, Mrs. Novak sends Mr. Novak out to the Courtneys' backyard.

MR. NOVAK Hi, guys.

MR. COURTNEY Hey, Joe, those tomatoes in your garden are beauties.

MR. NOVAK You're suddenly into horticulture, buddy? You haven't the patience to grow vegetables!

MR. COURTNEY I'm a city boy. No green thumb at all. That's why I have generous neighbors like you!

MR. NOVAK Okay, neighbor. I get the message. Tomatoes for dinner. Say, you're planning on sharing some of that steak, aren't you?

MR. COURTNEY You bet. Didn't Sue tell you? We're putting everything together and having a potluck.

MR. NOVAK Terrific! I'll go pick some ripe, juicy tomatoes.

MRS. NOVAK I'm back! Here are the heads of lettuce.

MRS. COURTNEY Great. We can make the salad now and chill it in a bowl over ice cubes in the sink.

SCENE 5

NARRATOR 2 Before long, the salad is made. The steaks and toast are finishing up on the grill under Mr. Courtney's watchful eye. The rest of the grownups enjoy hanging out on the patio and watching the kids play ball.

MRS. NOVAK Does anyone need any more lemonade?

MR. COURTNEY Sure. Thanks, Sue.

MR. NOVAK Me too. Thanks.

MRS. COURTNEY Ah, clothes on the line!

MRS. NOVAK Just like when I was little girl.

MRS. COURTNEY Dryers are great, but everything happens behind a little closed door. It's nice to watch sheets flapping in the wind. They make interesting shapes—like clouds. Maybe the old ways aren't so bad.

MRS. NOVAK When I was a girl, I loved lying in bed on Saturday mornings and hearing the vacuum cleaner downstairs. Of course, that was when it was my sister's turn to do the vacuuming.

MRS. COURTNEY On the other hand, maybe the old ways weren't so great! In our household today, everybody helps with housework—not just the girls. Bill will help me take down these clothes, and the kids all pitch in to do the folding.

MRS. NOVAK Three cheers for the girls—and guys—of today!

JESSICA (*shouting*) I caught it on a fly, you're out!

AMANDA So do you guys believe NOW we can be outfielders?!

BAE Hey, I'm convinced.

JUNG and TYLER Me too!

MRS. COURTNEY (*shouting*) Okay, ballplayers! Better stop for now and get cooled off. We're going to have dinner in a jiffy. Would any of you kids like to join us?

JUNG Thanks, Mrs. Courtney. I think we'd better go check with our mom first.

AMANDA Yeah, me too. I'll be back if I can.

MRS. COURTNEY Say, where is Will? I haven't seen him for a while. He'll miss supper!

SCENE 6

NARRATOR 3 Just then, Will comes around the corner of the house with a strange man who is holding a big shopping bag.

WILL Hey, everybody. I want you to meet Tito, the Tamale Man.

TYLER Oh! You're Tito, the Tamale Man from TV!

MR. PEREZ That's right. Of course, I have a real name—it's Tito Perez.

MRS. NOVAK You're famous! Everyone knows about your tamales.

MR. NOVAK We like them, don't we honey? They're delicious.

MR. PEREZ Thank you. I started out pushing a vendor cart on the streets of Detroit. Today, we ship our product all over the country.

WILL Mom and Dad, Mr. Perez is the one who moved into that big house down the block I watched being built.

MRS. COURTNEY Ah! The one you were wondering about, Will. Mystery solved!

MR. PEREZ I always thought I was a city boy, and that I'd miss it, but everyone in the suburbs seems so nice and friendly. You sure know how to throw a party.

MR. COURTNEY Well, Mr. Perez—Tito—we're very glad to have you for a neighbor. We're from Detroit too. You know, your name sounds familiar. Perez. I think I know you from somewhere.

MRS. COURTNEY The TV commercials, Honey.

MR. COURTNEY No, I mean more than that. Don't you have a brother named Diego?

TITO Well, yes, I do!

MR. COURTNEY I was on the soccer team with him at Wayne High School!

TYLER Dad, you were on the soccer team?

MR. COURTNEY Sure, kid! I was—er—in better shape then.

TITO Wow. After all these years. And I was on the team at New Claire High.

MR. COURTNEY Diego always talked about you.

TITO In fact, Diego is coming over later, if he can find his way in the dark.

MR. COURTNEY That guy could kick a ball into a goal in pitch-dark when we practiced on the high school fields after hours.

TITO I know. He'll find us.

MR. COURTNEY Maybe we can get a game going!

WILL Everybody, Mr. Perez has a whole bunch of tamales in that shopping bag.

JESSICA Just what are tamales? I mean, what are they made of?

TITO They're a special mixture of meat or vegetables wrapped up in corn husks. Some people use banana leaves. You never had a tamale before?

JESSICA No. But I'd sure like to try one.

TITO Great! Because I've got chicken, pork, vegetable—even cinnamon-chocolate dessert tamales. We can warm them up on the grill.

MR. COURTNEY Fantastic! Pull up a chair. We've got steaks, salad, and garlic toast. Let's put everything together and dig in!

ALL VOICES *(ad lib)* Sure! Sounds great. Yummy! Let's go!

SCENE 7

NARRATOR 4 The neighborhood party goes on after sunset. All the neighbors light candles on their picnic tables and torches on their patios.

DIEGO Tito! Tito! Are you there?

TITO Hola! Over here! Everybody, it's my brother Diego.

DIEGO Looks like you amigos are having a great party. What have I missed?

MR. COURTNEY Diego! Remember Wayne High? The soccer team? Your old buddy, Bill Courtney?

DIEGO I remember a really good runner named Bill Courtney. Is that you, man?

NARRATOR 1 And of course, for the next fifteen minutes, those two fading soccer stars share memories about the good old days.

NARRATOR 2 But then, suddenly . . .

MRS. COURTNEY Stop shining that flashlight in my face, Will.

WILL Mom, it's not a flashlight, the power's come back on.

MR. NOVAK Everyone's TVs are blaring.

MRS. NOVAK Yes, and they're drowning out our conversations.

MR. COURTNEY I guess we could all go back in now. But do you know what? I don't really want to.

TYLER Me neither, Dad. Let's go shut off the TVs and some of the lights.

WILL I'll help.

MR. COURTNEY Good idea, guys.

JESSICA Hey Mom?

MRS. COURTNEY Yes, Jessica?

JESSICA I don't think I want to go to California.

MRS. COURTNEY Giving up on surfing?

JESSICA I'm not giving up on it, but I didn't know we could have so much fun right here in our own backyards.

MRS. COURTNEY Someday we may still go to California on vacation.

JESSICA Could Amanda come along? Would you, Amanda?

AMANDA Oooh! I'd love that!

MRS. COURTNEY Sure, honey. I'm glad you two made friends today.

MR. COURTNEY Looks like we won't have to wait for a crisis to get you kids out of the house next time!

TYLER You bet, Dad! I had a super time playing ball with Jung, Bae, and the other kids today.

JUNG, BAE, and AMANDA *(ad lib)* Yeah! We did too! This was great!

JESSICA Who'd ever guess it would take a power outage to get to know our neighbors?!

Poetry Interpretation

To interpret poetry means to read it aloud for an audience. You use your voice, body, and facial expressions to get its meaning across. Basically, there are three types of poems.

A **dramatic poem** has speeches like dialogue. It is like a short play written in verse. To interpret it, first you need to identify who are the characters and what is their relationship to each other. Also determine what is the conflict between them and how it is resolved—if it is.

Some dramatic poems are written for one character only. Such a poem is a *monologue.* You still need to identify the character and the dramatic situation. Then ask: Is that character speaking to another character (who has no lines) or to himself or herself?

When you have analyzed the characters, you can act them out as you would act the characters in a play. The difference is that you may need to use two different character voices and perhaps shift your eye focus back and forth as you switch from character to character.

A **narrative poem** tells a story. You can use any of the elements of good storytelling to make the poem come alive for your audience. Usually the speaker is not a character, but in *Paul Revere's Ride,* the speaker begins, "Listen, my children, and you shall hear . . . ," rather like an old man gathering his grandchildren around him for a storytelling session.

A **lyric poem** expresses the speaker's thoughts or feelings. It may simply describe an interesting scene, or it may tell how the speaker has gone through emotional changes. It can be very personal, but the pronoun *I* in a lyric poem doesn't necessarily refer to the poet. The speaker may be playing a character, as in a dramatic monologue. To interpret a lyric poem, you need to identify—if you can—who is the speaker and what are the speaker's feelings about his or her surroundings.

WHAT DOES IT MEAN?

As an interpreter of poetry, your first job is to make the audience understand what is going on. To do that, you have to be sure you understand it yourself. Here are some pointers:

- *Understand every word.* Use a dictionary for any word you're not sure of. Think about the connotations (suggested meanings) of the words as well as their denotations (dictionary meanings). Also check any allusions, or references to characters or situations in myth, history, and so on.

- *Think about the title.* Is it descriptive? ironic? Does it suggest new meanings for the poem?

- *Study the structure.* Look for complete sentences. Use punctuation to help you know when to pause. Some poems are not structured in sentences. In that case, look for complete thoughts. Identifying a subject and verb might help. Think about ways you can use your voice to get across your understanding of the structure.

WHAT SHOULD IT SOUND LIKE?

After you understand the poem, you have to get your understanding across to your audience. Ask yourself these questions:

- *What is the style or mood of the poem?* Is it lighthearted, or dark and moody? Is it humorous or serious? Is it written in simple, everyday language or in more ornate "poetic" language?

- *What is the rhythm of the poem?* Does it call for a quick, light reading or a slow, thoughtful one? Be sure you stress the syllables in words that are stressed naturally in speech.

- *Does it rhyme?* The rhymes of a poem contribute to its overall impression. As an interpreter, usually you do not need to stress the rhymes. If you read for the sense, the rhymes may simply fall into place.

- *How about emphasis?* Some poems seem to call for a fairly even pace and emphasis throughout. Others may call for changes in volume or intensity to stress words, ideas, or images. Don't forget—a pause can emphasize too.

- *How can you phrase, or group words together, to express the sense of the poem?* You don't have to pause at the end of each line; in fact, it may destroy the sense if you try to do so. Experiment with different phrasings. Read for the punctuation, if that is helpful. Otherwise, read for the ideas.

YOUR PERFORMANCE

Practice your interpretation aloud several times before you perform it. If possible, practice in front of a mirror. You might also ask a classmate or family member to give you helpful feedback.

Be sure you know how to pronounce every word. Use a dictionary for any word you're not sure of. Practice the difficult words and difficult word combinations until you can say them smoothly without stumbling.

You don't have to memorize the poem you are reading. You should be familiar enough with it, though, that you can look up from your book or script to make eye contact with your audience. For a dramatic poem you may not want to make audience contact but instead look at a place where you imagine the characters to be.

Be sure to speak loudly enough that you can be heard all around the room—including the back row.

Take your time. When you step in front of your audience, don't rush into your performance. Take a few deep breaths and focus on the job you are doing. At the end, pause, look at your audience, and smile, to let them know your performance is finished.

Choral Reading

You can involve a small group or a whole class in poetry interpretation. This is not just a simple matter of a group reading aloud in unison. It can be a rich way to explore a poem with a wider variety of voice qualities than a single reader can bring to the work.

THE SCRIPT

First you need to decide who reads what lines; that is, to divide the lines among Readers 1, 2, 3, all male voices, all female voices, and so on. Your script is an orchestration in which a single voice or a combination of voices or the whole group might read a single line—or a single word. This scripting can be done by a director or by the group as a whole, but it might be more efficient to assign two or three members to do the job.

Use your imagination here. Voices can sound like animals or machines; they can wail or rejoice; they can sing, hum, and create a great variety of sound effects. Of course, all these noises must be appropriate for the poem you are interpreting.

REHEARSAL AND PERFORMANCE

Rehearsals are vital to an effective choral performance. They are perhaps best led by a director who signals individuals and groups when to come in. If there is no director, assign one strong reader to start off each choral section so that the rest of the group can come in immediately, giving the effect that they all started together. Have a signal so that the group can stop together too.

Plan your entrances and exits and where all the people stand or sit when they are not reading. Remember, even when you are not the one reading, you are still onstage. You must do your part to direct the audience's attention by keeping your focus on the ones who are reading.

The Brave Ones

by Eloise Greenfield

We hear the bell clanging
we come in a hurry
we come with our ladders and hoses
our hoses
we come in a hurry
to fight the fire
the furious fire
to smother the smoke
the smoke
we don't have much time
we climb, we spray
we are the brave ones who save
who save
we are the brave ones who save

Mr. Nobody

Anonymous

I know a funny little man,
    As quiet as a mouse,
Who does the mischief that is done
    In everybody's house!
There's no one ever sees his face,
    And yet we all agree
That every plate we break was cracked
    By Mr. Nobody.

'Tis he who always tears our books,
    Who leaves the door ajar,
He pulls the buttons from our shirts,
    And scatters pins afar;
That squeaking door will always squeak,
    For, prithee, don't you see,
We leave the oiling to be done
    By Mr. Nobody.

He puts damp wood upon the fire,
    That kettles cannot boil;
His are the feet that bring in mud,
    And all the carpets soil.
The papers always are mislaid,
    Who had them last but he?
There's no one tosses them about
    But Mr. Nobody.

The finger marks upon the door
    By none of us are made;
We never leave the blinds unclosed,
    To let the curtains fade.
The ink we never spill; the boots
    That lying round you see
Are not our boots—they all belong
    To Mr. Nobody.

---

prithee I pray thee; please [Archaic]

How to Assemble a Toy

by John Ciardi

This is the whatsit that fits on the knob
Of the gadget that turns the thingamabob.
This is the dingus that fits in place
With the doodad next to the whosiface.
This is the jigger that goes in the hole
Where the gizmo turns the rigamarole.
Now slip the ding-dang into the slot
Of the jugamalug, and what have you got?

It's a genuine neverwas such a not!

Unit 3 Inventors and Artists

The Basket Weaver

by Carole Boston Weatherford

She wades the marshlands and gathers grass
to weave the baskets that hold her past.
She coils sea grass with palmetto frond.
Her timeless art forms tribal bonds.

The craft she learned at her mama's knee,
her forebears brought across the sea.
Baskets sewn with skill by slaves
held grains of rice, and cradled babes.

With pride aglow on her ebony face,
she sells her wares at the marketplace.
The baskets she still weaves by hand
hold memories of the Motherland.

Unit 4 Adapting

Changing
by Mary Ann Hoberman

I know what I feel like;
I'd like to be *you*
And feel what *you* feel like
And do what *you* do.
I'd like to change places
For maybe a week
And look like your look-like
And speak as you speak
And think what you're thinking
And go where you go
And feel what you're feeling
And know what you know.
I wish we could do it;
What fun it would be
If I could try you out
And you could try me.

Early Explorers

by Marilyn Singer

No Place on earth

    is ever undiscovered

Even in Antarctica

    where whole mountains are hidden

      under ice

penguins already laid shambling tracks

      in the snow

    before we traveled there

The hottest desert

      the deepest jungle

    where none of us have ever been

all have been crossed

      and crossed again

    by wings whirring or silent

      feet furred or scaled

        hoofed or bare

By adventurers we will never know

    explorers who will never tell us

      what wonders they have seen

Always Take a Dog

by Joyce Sidman

Go out walking.
In some part of every day,
step into the waiting arms
of the sky and whisk away—
but always take a dog,
so that you have something to follow.

Stroll or saunter,
steam up hills, thoughts rumbling
through your head like bees
bent on their own courses—
but always take a dog,
so you can watch how he chooses
which path to take.

Absorb the light:
the sun-splayed distance,
the close, soft dampness
of a cloudy day—
but always take a dog,
so you can see how
the wind moves through his fur.

Be alert for what the day
might offer you; a gull, a penny,
the pale thumbprint of moon—
but always take a dog,
so you can heed how
his nose moves from side to side,
seeking unexpected treasure.

Unit 6 The Unexpected

He Thought He Saw

by Lewis Carroll

He thought he saw a Buffalo
    Upon the chimney-piece;
He looked again, and found it was
    His Sister's Husband's Niece.
"Unless you leave this house," he said,
    "I'll send for the Police!"

He thought he saw a Rattlesnake
    That questioned him in Greek;
He looked again, and found it was
    The Middle of Next Week.
"The one thing I regret," he said,
    "Is that it cannot speak!"

He thought he saw a Banker's Clerk
    Descending from the bus;
He looked again, and found it was
    A Hippopotamus.
"If this should stay to dine," he said,
    "There won't be much for us!"

(continued on next page)

He Thought He Saw

(continued)

He thought he saw a Kangaroo
    That worked a coffee-mill;
He looked again, and found it was
    A Vegetable-Pill.
"Were I to swallow this," he said,
    "I should be very ill!"

He thought he saw a Coach-and-Four
    That stood beside his bed;
He looked again, and found it was
    A Bear without a Head.
"Poor thing," he said, "poor silly thing!
    It's waiting to be fed!"

He thought he saw an Albatross
    That fluttered round the lamp;
He looked again, and found it was
    A Penny-Postage-Stamp.
"You'd best be getting home," he said,
    "The nights are very damp!"

---

coach-and-four a horse-drawn carriage and the team of four horses
    that pull it
albatross a large, web-footed bird found chielfy in the South Seas

Tests About Poetry

Multiple-Choice Test

When you take a multiple-choice test, you can think about the choices to be sure that you choose the best ones. Read the poem and answer the questions that follow in the left column. Then, in the right column, read some ways you might think about the choices in questions 1–4.

I Meant to Do My Work Today
by Richard LeGallienne

I meant to do my work today—
But a brown bird sang in the apple tree,
And a butterfly flitted across the field,
And all the leaves were calling me.

And the wind went sighing over the land
Tossing the grasses to and fro,

And a rainbow held out its shining hand—
So what could I do but laugh and go?

Test Question

1. What is the mood of the poem?
   - **A** happy
   - **B** sad
   - **C** angry
   - **D** worried

Answering the Question

Question 1 The speaker isn't sad, because he or she laughs, so answer *B* is not correct. The speaker doesn't seem angry or worried because he or she is enjoying different elements of nature, so answers *C* and *D* are not correct. But the speaker does laugh and go off to enjoy the day instead of working, so answer *A* must be correct.

Test Question	Answering the Question

2. The lines *But a brown bird sang in the apple tree* and *And all the leaves were calling me* provide an example of what poetic device?

A onomatopoeia

B stanza

C idiom

D rhyme

Question 2 There aren't any words in these lines that sound like their meanings, so answer *A* (onomatopoeia) is not correct. There isn't really a good example of an idiom, or a phrase with a special meaning, in the poem, so answer *C* is not correct. There are two stanzas, or verses, in the poem, but these two lines are only part of the first stanza, so answer *B* is not the best answer. But the words *tree* and *me* do rhyme, or share the same ending sound, so answer *D* must be correct.

3. Which technique does the poet use in the phrase *a rainbow held out its shining hand?*

A simile

B personification

C metaphor

D alliteration

Question 3 There is no comparison in the quoted phrase, either with the words *like* or *as* or without them, so answers *A* (simile) and *C* (metaphor) are not correct. There is no alliteration, or repetition of initial sounds, so answer *D* is not correct. But talking about a rainbow that has a hand is giving that rainbow a human trait, so answer *B* (personification) must be correct.

4. What is the theme of the poem?

A You can't always do what you want to do.

B The singing of birds is beautiful.

C There are some things more important than work.

D We must take care not to destroy our world.

Question 4 The speaker *does* do what he or she wants to do, so answer *A* cannot be correct. The bird's singing may be beautiful, but that is not what the whole poem is about, so answer *B* is not correct. The statement in answer *D* may be true, but it is not dealt with in the poem, so that is not correct. But the idea that the speaker does not do his or her work, but goes off to enjoy the day, suggests that answer *C* is the best answer.

Writing Test

Read the poem and then follow the directions to write your responses. When you write answers to a test question, you can think about your answers to be sure that they express your understanding. In the right column are some ways you might think about questions 5–7. (Some answers have been filled in as examples.)

Celebration
by Alonzo Lopez

I shall dance tonight.
When the dusk comes crawling,
There will be dancing
   and feasting.
I shall dance with the others
   in circles,
     in leaps,
      in stomps.

Laughter and talk
   will weave into the night,
Among the fires
   of my people.
Games will be played
And I shall be
   a part of it.

Test Question	Answering the Question
5. Use details from the poem to fill in the boxes below.	**Question 5** Do the words you have chosen come from the poem? Do they provide good examples of what the question asks for (the heads in the box)?

What the Speaker Does to Celebrate

dance, dancing, feasting, circles, leaps, stomps

Words That Show the Speaker Is Not Alone

the others, my people

6. Write a word of your own to tell how the speaker feels.	**Question 6** Does your word honestly express what you think the speaker feels?

belonging

Now read this poem and then follow the directions to write your response. Look at the footnotes to be sure you understand all the words.

I'm Nobody

by Emily Dickinson

I'm nobody! Who are you?
Are you nobody, too?
Then there's a pair of us—don't tell!
They'd banish us, you know.

How dreary to be somebody!
How public, like a frog
To tell your name the livelong day
To an admiring bog!

---

banish to force to leave a country or go away
dreary gloomy
bog an area of soft, wet ground, such as a swamp

Test Question	Answering the Question
7. Think about the speaker in "Celebration" and the speaker in "I'm Nobody." How are these speakers different? Use a word of your own to describe each speaker and explain why you have chosen these words. Use examples from BOTH poems to support your answer.	**Question 7** Read the question carefully to be sure you understand what you are to write. Here, you are to do two things: describe the two speakers and contrast them. This question also provides a checklist for you to be sure your answer is a complete one. After you have written your answer, be sure to check it against this list.

In your answer, be sure to

- tell how the speakers in the poems are different

- use a word to describe each speaker and explain why you have chosen this word

- use examples from BOTH poems